PASTORAL CARE FOR
LONELINESS

PASTORAL CARE FOR LONELINESS

A New Apostolate

MATTHEW FFORDE

GRACEWING

La pastorale della solitudine. Una nuova proposta
first published by Edizioni Cantagalli in 2020

English version by the author

First published in England in 2023
by
Gracewing
2 Southern Avenue
Leominster
Herefordshire HR6 0QF
United Kingdom
www.gracewing.co.uk

ISBN 978 085244 993 6

Typeset by Gracewing
Cover design by Bernardita Peña Hurtado

To all those who convert their
suffering into helping others

Our time is marked by individualism and indifference, which generate loneliness and lead to the throwing away of many lives. This is our culture today. Individualism, indifference, which generate loneliness and cause rejection: the throwaway culture.

Pope Francis, *Address to the Camillians,* 16 May 2022

CONTENTS

PREFACE

THE COVID-19 CRISIS, with its preventive measures of self-isolation on a massive scale, has called attention to another contemporary scourge—the epidemic of loneliness. In this case, isolation imposed not by health-care guidelines but by dysfunctional cultural conditions. 'Social distancing' has been underway on another front and with increasing intensity. It is my hope that the coronavirus crisis will sensitise people to the presence and characteristics of this parallel plague. However, this essay (indeed a manifesto)[1] has its roots that go back before 2020 and is the result of many years of troubled thought about the epidemic of loneliness in various forms that is sweeping through Western societies. We are now faced not so much with 'liquid modernity' as 'lonely modernity'. In my work *Desocialisation. The Crisis of Post-Modernity*, published over a decade ago, I sought to set out an analysis of the causes and character of this epidemic, taking Great Britain as an example of the crisis now afflicting Western man. In this work I again draw upon the British model when discussing the empirical features of this crisis but readers from other nations will here readily recognise phenomena that are afflicting their societies as well. In this short volume I offer one response that Christians could adopt to this scourge and it is in the first instance addressed to Catholic clergy, religious Orders, associations and lay faithful. Indeed, this essay seeks to contribute to a nascent debate within Catholicism about what Christians could do about this epidemic of our times. I hope, however, that this work will also appeal to our Christian brothers and sisters not of the Catholic tradition (contributing to an 'ecumenism of works') and to men and women of good will of other religions or of no religion at all, and thus be a way of linking up with them in a common action of healing and relieving suffering.

The project of pastoral care for loneliness was first launched in an ecclesial context in the Archdiocese of Crotone-Santa Severina, Calabria. On 18–19 January 2019 a symposium in that archdiocese was held to debate what this new form of pastoral care could be and how it could be developed. I would like to acknowledge the contribution made to this essay by the thoughts of the Archbishop, clergy and lay faithful of that archdiocese expressed during that symposium. This work bears the imprint of their practical wisdom.

I would also like to thank the students of my courses at my university, LUMSA, in Rome, who over the decades have offered me important insights—from the perspective of young people—into the phenomenon of the breakdown of social ties so characteristic of post-modernity. Many friends and colleagues have made comments on the project that this essay seeks to advance, or on this text, in truth far too many to mention here, but especial thanks must go to Karen Andrews, Gian Filippo Belardo, Vitaliano Dati, Clarisse Faugeron, the late Peter Ivens, Noemi Maas-Dagan, Thomas McEnchroe and William McEnchroe for their input. In addition, as I look back I realise how much I owe to a variety of figures who helped me on my way—often intervening at key points of difficulty—and enabled me to reach the point where I could offer this text to readers. Of course, I am entirely responsible for the inevitable inadequacies of this text which is the work of somebody who does not have the practical experience of working in the front line of ministry. I dedicate this volume to all those who convert their suffering into helping others.

MF
Rome, August 2022

Notes

1   It may be necessary to issue a second manifesto, after pastoral care for loneliness has been implemented, which would gather together the lessons that have been learnt about what the configurations and contours of this new form of pastoral care should be.

1 A TIME TO ACT

GOD DECLARED 'IT is not good that man should be alone' (Gn 2:18) but a spectre is now haunting Western societies: the spectre of loneliness. In January 2018 the British government announced that it was appointing a sort of roving 'minister' to address the question of loneliness—a telling indicator of just how bad things have become.[1] Everywhere we look we are faced with a growing loss of social ties and the imposition of alienation, separation and isolation. 'One of the deepest forms of poverty a person can experience is isolation', observed Benedict XVI, 'Man is alienated when he is alone'.[2] The results are before all our eyes: our contemporaries are increasingly sick in a variety of forms from being increasingly on their own. Given the dynamics, we have probably seen nothing yet. Do we really want to move towards a post-social future? Looking at possible distant horizons, do we really want to turn our Western societies into open-air prisons made up of solitary confinement cells? Christians are always called to read the 'signs of the times'[3] and in the spread of loneliness in the West we encounter a sign of dramatic proportions. As regards this dark aspect of where post-modernity has led us, enough is enough. Urgent action is now required—this is a time to act. In following Christ who in his ministry here on earth cured people of their afflictions and ordered his disciples to do likewise (Lk 9:2), and told us that in helping the afflicted we would help him (Mt 25:35–40), Christians are now called to heal Western man of this epidemic of our epoch and to relieve the suffering that it imposes. This short work seeks to contribute to this undertaking by launching a new initiative, a new social ministry, a new form of pastoral care—pastoral care for loneliness (PCL). How beautiful it would be if after our deaths Christ could say to us: "I was lonely, I suffered because of it, and you kept me company".

This manifesto is primarily aimed at Catholicism and invites its over a billion adherents in the world to place pastoral care for loneliness at the side of the other forms of pastoral care that have been developed down the centuries. In this, it necessarily aims at consciousness-raising amongst the faithful about loneliness and what should be done about it. Within the Catholic Church it has been recognised that different areas deserve their own special kinds of pastoral care. One may think of pastoral care for the sick, for the family, for young people, for the dying or for the bereaved. PCL can draw upon these traditions in shaping its character and at times interact with them, thereby developing and strengthening the pastoral aspect of what Catholicism is and should be. But this project also aims at those outside the Catholic world, seeking, for example, cooperation with the other Christian denominations. This is because in addressing loneliness and all its suffering we are addressing a *human* problem, the evil of which is recognised by all men and women of good will because of their humanity. You do not have to belong to one specific outlook to be moved by compassion at the pain of those who find themselves isolated against their will. Indeed, cooperation between Catholics and people of other outlooks in helping those who suffer from loneliness will be a way of building bridges and stressing affinities.

However, this project is a direct appeal to Catholics in the first instance, and for a number of principal reasons. Firstly, Christ explicitly called his followers to engage in healing and the relief of pain. There are two dimensions to this. On the one hand, he constantly cured people of their physical and spiritual maladies. He was the physician of bodies and souls. He directly invited his disciples to imitate him in this ministry and sent out his disciples with exactly such a mandate. It is no surprise, in this context, that the history of Christianity has been marked by the known and unknown work of so many people dedicated to caring for and healing the sick. On the other, Christ declared that those who visit his brothers and sisters who are ill visit him and that to do such is to be blessed. Imposed loneliness is a malady and thus Christians are called to counter its existence and its consequences by divine commandment. At the same time, those Christians who help and comfort their brothers and sisters who suffer its realities are helping and comforting Christ himself in those people.

Related to this is the fact that to help those who are lonely is an act of love for neighbour which in itself can only conduce to the spiritual wellbeing, to the health of the souls, of those who practise it. To do good does good to its practitioner. Christ invited his followers to achieve spiritual health by implementing the commandment of love. Pastoral care for loneliness is a contemporary imperative need that offers a pathway for such an implementation. At the same time, it provides an opportunity for those who have suffered from loneliness to draw upon their own experiences in order to help others who are afflicted by the same malaise. This manifesto, therefore, makes a special appeal to Christians who have been, or are, lonely, to contribute what they know about dealing with this condition to the development of a kind of pastoral care that seeks to combat this condition. In this way, what they have gone through will not have been in vain and they can transform it into a force for good: *ex malo bonum* (a very evangelical notion). Lead can be transmuted into gold.

In addition, at a time, especially in the West, when Christian culture has been retreating fast, it offers Christians a special way by which to reaffirm their identity and convince people of the validity of their beliefs; they can be helped in carrying their evangelical lanterns in this secularist storm. This can take place within the context of the Catholic Church's invocation of a new evangelisation which is a clear recognition of this retreat. In his ministry on earth, Christ linked healing to the spread of the Gospel; curing people of their ills was a way of establishing credibility for his message. The restoration of health involved a call to faith. His followers now have an opportunity to carry on this approach. In developing pastoral care for loneliness, in helping people who suffer from the consequences of loneliness, Christians will bear witness to their faith by seeking to bring healing. In striving to cure people who suffer from this scourge of our time, they will make what they are, and what they believe in, more credible. Pastoral care for loneliness will offer the followers of Christ an opportunity to make his message more persuasive and convincing through countering the malaise of people's absence of social ties. In reviving and regenerating those who are disaggregated, Christians can revive and regenerate the lineage to which they belong. A unique opportunity presents itself for a promotion of the gospel through a very special kind of healing and care which constitutes authentic witness to faith. DeChristianisation can be reversed by coming to the aid of those at the side of the road who have not been robbed and beaten by brigands (cf. Lk 10:30) but ignored, marginalised and abandoned by their fellows.

Furthermore, there is much to indicate that the epidemic of loneliness that is now sweeping the West, and perhaps on its way to becoming one of the great issues of our time, is closely connected with the decline of Christian culture in our civilisation. It is highly suggestive that the 'desocialisation' of Western man has greatly intensified as a phenomenon over recent decades at exactly the same time as secularisation has become ever more powerful. The chronology is highly suggestive. Indeed, Western countries are now experiencing two unprecedented phenomena and they appear to be intimately bound up: a widespread lack of religious faith and huge amounts of people living alone. It is almost as if we have turned our backs on the central truths of the New Testament (and not only of the New Testament) and have adopted ways of thinking about the universe, man, society, culture, ethics and morals that build walls between people. As Christian culture has retreated, what has leapt into its place has worked against man (in particular the idea that we do not have a soul and truth is relative). The central idea of love for neighbour, which is a gigantic engine for bringing people together, has been replaced by other ideas that seem to have the opposite effect. In engaging in an attempt to heal Western man of his loneliness, Christians, from a historical perspective, will be seeking to counter the consequences of beliefs, notions and ways of understanding that have attacked the gospel message and its integrating effects. Pastoral care for loneliness can be a direct way by which Christians can help to repair the damage caused by a sustained assault on the axioms of their culture.

An authentic Christian sensibility is marked by a special sensitivity to the pain and suffering of others. Christ's ministry on earth was characterised by his compassion for those he encountered who were afflicted. His healings and

his preaching involved an attempt to remove such afflic-
tion and he asked his disciples to follow his example.
Compassion, indeed, forms a part of the nobility of man
and those who do not feel compassion should always be
regarded with great suspicion. Christians, therefore,
should be especially sensitive to the gigantic levels of
suffering (often of a hidden kind) that are now generated
by loneliness and should be moved to act because of this
sensitivity. Every Sunday, every Easter and every Christ-
mas, the West is full of the silent suffering of those who
in one way or another do not have others near to them.
Do we not want to listen to this unexpressed weeping? The
hidden cries of those out on their own constitute calls to
which the followers of Christ cannot be indifferent—quite
the contrary. They cannot pass by on the other side of the
road (cf. Lk 10:31–2). Their vocation is to help; here we
encounter true solidarity.

In addition, there is the whole dimension of hope.
Believing in divine intervention, Christians are constantly
called to hope. *Spes contra spem.* The situation in the West
as regards the isolation of contemporary man is now more
than daunting. Coming to the effective aid of the disaggregated and countering what has happened would appear a
gigantic—perhaps even impossible—task; the North Face
of the Eiger in a different guise. Yet believing in transcen-
dental help—and placing faith in the enormous potential
for good of people—Christians can face up to this task with
confidence. Indeed, the Church can bring this hope to those
who suffer isolation against their will. Moreover, there is
good reason to believe that an initiative to care for the
lonely will have an accelerating effect: the more it is seen to
work, the more it will be adopted; the more cure is achieved,
the more it will be effective. Loneliness frequently involves
an absence of what there should be, a lack of love, affection,

company and civic friendship, but with faith we can be assured that contemporary man will not be destroyed by the void. This essay, therefore, is a message of hope because it maintains that for those who believe, and for those who believe in good, hope will be a continuous source of strength. As for myself, after all these decades, they will have to carry me out in a coffin before I surrender.

This new social ministry is also most suited to Catholicism because it can act as a unifying force within its ranks. The Catholic Church is a 'broad church' of different traditions, lineages, outlooks, emphases and nuances, not least because of its varying geographical and cultural locations. But all these examples of diversity can unite behind the imperative to provide help to the lonely, just as they unite, for example, behind the imperative to provide help to the sick. PCL, therefore, can not only help to build bridges with forces outside the Catholic Church, it can also act as a cohering and harmonising force within it. And is not unity strength?

Pastoral care for loneliness promoted by Catholics can gain special inspiration from the magisterium of Pope Francis. A recurrent theme of his thinking has been the need to work against what he refers to as a 'throwaway' or 'waste' culture.[4] Certainly one can see the millions of people condemned to isolation and loneliness as examples of individuals who are ignored and disregarded—'thrown away'; at the same time they are rich resources for our societies that are simply 'wasted'. In responding to the appeal of the Supreme Pontiff, we can engage in an authentic exercise of true social integration of those who have been 'discarded' by processes beyond their control. Equally, the Pope has talked about the need to bring care and help to the fringes.[5] Do we not in Western societies have, in a metaphorical sense, thickly populated fringes inhabited by people who are very much out on their own? In another area of thought (political correctness), great emphasis is placed on being 'inclusive' with a concomitant call for the integration of 'diversity'. The great question, of course, is what groups form a part of this project. Should this line of thinking not also be applied to the lonely, with their inclusion considered an impelling priority?

Pope Francis has also called for an 'outward bound Church'.[6] Pastoral care for loneliness is a way of responding to this appeal and of moving towards those in need. In this age when Christian culture in the West has retreated and is still under major attack there is a temptation for its adherents to withdraw into a comfort zone of routine activity, to retreat to a castle behind a drawbridge in the face of a hostile environment. The agents of this new form of pastoral care must resist this temptation and must not only engage in activity amongst the faithful—they must reach out to those who need help, whoever and wherever they may be. Indeed, the lonely are often hidden and not readily visible. St Camillus de Lellis, who developed pastoral care for the sick and the dying at the end of the sixteenth century, used to wander through the streets of Rome to find sick people to look after and encouraged those who worked with him to do the same. This example of outward movement animated by the heart—this patron saint of the sick often enjoined his followers to 'put more heart in those hands'—shines down to us down the centuries.

Pastoral care for loneliness is primarily intended for the secularised West, and in particular for the anglosphere, northern Europe and their great urban conurbations, for here loneliness is conspicuous by its presence. In 2016 Cardinal Parolin, the Secretary of State of the Vatican, referred to:

A form of poverty present even in those countries
and families that are less poor, even in people
belonging to categories that have access to means
and opportunities, but which experience the inner
emptiness of having lost meaning and direction in
life, or who are violently struck by the desolation
of broken bonds, of the harshness of loneliness, or
the feeling of being forgotten by all or of not being
of use to anyone.[7]

It is therefore to the inhabitants of these parts of the globe
that this essay is chiefly directed. However, all the signs
are that this scourge of our epoch will continue to spread
both in the West and beyond (accompanied by the expor-
tation of the idea that man does not have a soul, that truth
is 'relative', and that 'gender' is not a biological reality:
'ideological colonisation',[8] to employ the phrase of Pope
Francis). From this point of view, this manifesto is also an
invitation to people in areas not yet so harshly afflicted to
engage in preparatory and defensive work, perhaps even
prevention, in anticipation of what is to come. It is a call
to arms to those not yet severely attacked; to be fore-
warned is to be forearmed.

Notes

1   *The Guardian*, 16 January 2018, 'May Appoints Minister to Tackle Loneliness Issues Raised by Jo Cox'.

2   Pope Benedict XVI, *Caritas in veritate*, 53.

3   Vatican Council II, *Gaudium et Spes*, 4: 'the Church has always had the duty of scrutinizing the signs of the times and of interpreting them in the light of the Gospel'.

4   See, for example, Pope Francis, *General Audience* (5 June 2013); *Address at the Conclusion of Luncheon with the Participants in the International Seminar on the Pope's Proposal "Towards a More Inclusive Economy" Made in the Apostolic Exhortation Evangelii Gaudium* (12 July 2014); *Message to the Executive Chairman of the "World Economic Forum" on the Occasion of the Annual Gathering in Davos-Klosters* (12 January 2018) (available on the Holy See web site).

5   See, for example, Pope Francis, *Evangelii Gaudium*, 20; *Message for the Twenty-Ninth World Youth Day 2014* (21 January 2014); *To the Members of the National Association of Italian Municipalities (ANCI)* (30 September 2017) (available on the Holy See web site).

6   See, for example, Pope Francis, *Address to the Emmanuel Community* (7 April 2018) (available on the Holy See web site).

7   Cardinal P. Parolin, *Thanksgiving Mass for the Canonisation of Mother Teresa: Eyes Open to Suffering, Embraced with Compassion* (5 September 2016) bulletin of the Holy See Press Office (available on Internet).

8   See, for example, Pope Francis, Apostolic Journey to Sri Lanka and the Philippines (12–19 January 2015). *Address to Families* (16 January 2015) (available on the Holy See web site).

2 OUR CALL TO COMMUNITY

H UMANS HAVE A vocation to community. God himself is not alone and we should be like him. The Holy Trinity of God the Father, God the Son and God the Holy Spirit, a divine union of love, constitutes a model of social ties that man himself is called to imitate according to his human capacities. Christ asked his followers to strive for perfection: 'be perfect, just as your heavenly Father is perfect' (Mt 5:48) and the Father is perfect in his union with the other divine persons. Christ also preached that we should love our neighbour (and love truth) as we should love God, as he did. Therefore, in sustaining a human community of love and truth, we respond to what we are called to be as humans and we engage in an imitation of Christ. As the *Catechism of the Catholic Church* declares:

> The vocation of man is to show forth the image of God and to be transformed into the image of the Father's only Son ... This vocation takes a personal form since each of us is called to enter into the divine beatitude; it also concerns the human community as a whole ...

> All men are called to the same end: God himself. There is a certain resemblance between the union of the divine persons and the fraternity that men are to establish among themselves in truth and love. Love of neighbour is inseparable from love for God.

> The human person needs to live in society. Society is not for him an extraneous addition but a require-

ment of his nature. Through the exchange with
others, mutual service and dialogue with his breth-
ren, man develops his potential; he thus responds
to his vocation.

A *society* is a group of persons bound together
organically by a principle of unity that goes beyond
each one of them. As an assembly that is at once
visible and spiritual, a society endures through time;
it gathers up the past and prepares for the future.[1]

In Christian teaching man is seen as having (indeed being)
an immortal soul—this is his primary identity. Christ
taught that we should express love for love and for truth
(that is to say, bestow upon them supreme value) in our
relationships with other people (in adopting such a stance
towards others we also adopt it in relation to God) and
that this conduces to the health of our souls. Furthermore,
spiritual health in its turn naturally produces such love.
As love for love and for truth are the essential components
of community at every level, this teaching was also a call
for social union. Equally, spiritual health avoids the dark
side of man's being—the vices—that necessarily works
against such union and authentic social ties. At the same
time, the culture of a society (which is a moral entity all of
its own and in being human inevitably has a spiritual
content)[2] should itself generate this love for love and for
truth through its impact on individuals and not work in
the opposite direction. When Christ called for the advance
of the Kingdom of God amongst us, he was referring to
love for love and for truth expressed by individuals and by
a culture. Indeed, real community can only exist where
this primacy is at work—this is man's vocation for authentic life and achieves community with God. Alignment is
achieved with him and his kingdom is entered into. To go
against this vocation, to ignore the truths of Christ's

teachings, to neglect the wellbeing of our souls and of our culture, to go against divine law (and to promote another kingdom—let us remember that hell is perfect desociali-sation)[3] is to court disaster. We risk massive disorder in the way we live as individuals and as a society.

But the call to community through love for love and for truth is not only to be read in spiritual terms. It is also implicit in our biological nature as humans. There is general agreement on the intense sociability of *homo sapiens* and his need to live in a familiar and accessible setting of face-to-face relationships. The anthropologist M. Harris tells us: 'it is human nature to be the animal that is most dependent on social traditions for its survival and well-being'.[4] This evident sociability of man is borne out by what happens when it is systematically assaulted. Down the ages those engaged in the business of torture have well known the deeply destructive effects of solitary confine-ment. But it is not only this extreme condition that throws light on what we are. At a wider level, we know that man needs close ties for his wellbeing and inner stability. 'Individuals are not able to function effectively without deep links to others', observes A. Etzioni, 'without deep, continuous, and meaningful bonds, individuals risk losing their humanity'.[5] A positive shared culture (customs, traditions, ideas, institutions, language, ethics and morals) forms a part of the satisfaction of this need. As Isaiah Berlin observed: 'When men complain of loneliness, what they mean is that nobody understands what they are saying: to be understood is to share ... common forms of life'.[6] Panda bears may like the solitary life; human beings have rather different preferences. Good and effective community, sustained by a constructive common culture, is essential to us. If we are denied it, we become negated and run very great risks.

Notes

1   *Catechism of the Catholic Church* (London: Geoffrey Chapman, 1994), p. 413.

2   For an explanation of this unfashionable concept see M. Fforde, *Desocialisation. The Crisis of Post-Modernity* (Cheadle Hulme: Gabriel, 2009), pp. 30–36, 'The Soul and Culture'.

3   Is it not significant that the etymology of 'Devil' refers to the one who divides (διάβολος, *diábolos*)?

4   M. Harris, *Culture, People, Nature. An Introduction to General Anthropology* (New York: Harper and Row, 1980), p. 66.

5   A. Etzioni, *An Immodest Agenda. Rebuilding America before the Twenty-First Century* (New York: New Press, 1983), p. 29.

6   C. J. Calipeau, *Isaiah Berlin's Liberalism* (Oxford: Clarendon Press, 1994), p. 149.

3 THE NEGATION OF CONTEMPORARY MAN

OCIETIES OF THE Western world have been afflicted in recent decades by a massive decline in social ties at many levels and the growth of the epidemic of loneliness in all its forms. This has gone against what we are called to be as humans and is causing huge levels of malaise: contemporary man is being negated. What has been termed the 'progress' of our civilisation is in fact often a terrible regression. To affirm otherwise is to engage in denial. Nonetheless, this is precisely what many members of the power classes and exponents of dominant currents of thought often do; perhaps they do not want to acknowledge their possible responsibility for what has happened. Great Britain, during the modern age a pioneering nation which has often anticipated processes that were later to work themselves out in other countries in the West (and beyond), may be taken as an example of this 'desocialisation' of modern man.[1] The United Kingdom may be seen as a laboratory for developments that have been spreading far and wide. We are clearly dealing with an overall movement that has intensified since the 1960s; at times, what appears to be a veritable juggernaut. Given many of the trends, there is much to indicate that we may have seen nothing yet: decadence has the propensity to be an accelerating process. Here a brief survey of *key* indicators may suffice but a series of other phenomena could also be invoked. We appear to have on our hands an authentic 'cultural crisis'; a society disaggregating from within because the internal mechanisms that ensure cohesion have been severely weakened.

The institution of the family is in very serious trouble: divorce rates have climbed; the number of adults marrying has decreased; cohabitations, which some propose as an alternative to marriage, have risen rapidly, although prove even more unstable than marriage; and the decline in the nuclear family has been matched by a retreat of the wider family. Given these realities, it is not surprising that whereas in 1961 12% of households in Great Britain were made up of one person, by 2010 this had jumped to 29%.[2] By 2010 there were 7.5 million people living alone in the United Kingdom (55% of whom under the age of 65, an increase from 53% in 2001),[3] near to a third of the adult population and about four times as many as in 1961.[4] Something on this scale has never happened before in history. There is also the whole question of the lack of provision of love, affection and guidance by both parents to their children. 'A quarter of our children live with one parent, not two', it was observed in 2011, 'the absence of fathers in the lives of three quarters of a million children has become one of the major factors in the disaggregation of our communities'.[5] In this overall context, it is hardly surprising that recent years have witnessed the rise of a new genre of writing concerned with the traumas and horrors of childhoods lacking (to say the least) in bonds of love—'misery literature'. With the decline of the family, the ability (and propensity) to apply a familial culture of 'giving', 'looking after' and 'responsibility' to relationships outside the family has also been weakened, with results that are predictable but hard to measure.

There has also been a major increase in crime rates—and this includes violent crime rates—over the last fifty years,[6] a strong indicator of diminishing social cohesion.

In this context, it comes as no surprise that the prison population of England and Wales was at an all-time high at the beginning of the third millennium.[7] One testimony to this climate of violence, which takes a whole host of forms, is the fact that by 2003 it was estimated that one women in every four in England and Wales had experienced domestic violence at some time during her life.[8] 'Murder, knife crime and gun offences soared in England and Wales last year',[9] a national newspaper wrote in 2018; in early 2019 the BBC reported that recorded violent crime rates had increased by nearly 20% in England and Wales in 2018.[10] There is also the massive rise of what has been called 'anti-social behaviour' (vandalism, public drunkenness, drug usage and dealing, teenagers hanging around on the streets, etc.), another strong indicator of diminishing social cohesion.[11] A report of University College, London, of 2006 observed that the 'UK has the worst problem with anti-social behaviour in Europe'.[12]

Such developments have been paralleled by a huge fall in the legitimacy and prestige of political institutions, political parties and politicians (and this in a country which led the world in democratisation and whose national institutions were an important focus point for a sense of belonging), with an accompanying decline in participation in, and direct contacts with, the traditional political process. Opinion polls have indicated a collapse of trust in politicians; the membership of political parties is nothing compared to what it was in the 1950s; the two principal political parties, which once commanded a near hegemony at the polls and were deeply rooted national institutions, have experienced major declines in their proportion of the vote; and general elections have witnessed significant falls in turnout (going below 60% in 2001 and still below 68% in 2019; in 1950 the figure was

83.9%). In July 2018 the findings of one opinion poll were reported as indicating a 'crisis of faith in democracy', with widespread lack of trust in the elected representatives of different layers of government and a lack of direct contact between voters and their representatives. 40% of those interviewed had no trust at all (37% had little trust) that members of the House of Commons would do the right thing by them if contacted on an issue of any kind.[13] Overall, an increasing gap has grown up between the governed and their governors; a 'disconnect' between the rulers and the ruled. This development at an international level is one of the reasons for the rise in many Western societies in recent years (and Brexit was a good example of this in the UK)[14] of 'anti-establishment' feeling and what are termed 'populist' movements.

Reference should also be made to the apparent hollowing of civil society: we seem to have been experiencing a move away from traditional participatory membership and face-to-face interaction; direct ties here have also been debilitated. One may point to the decrease in membership of political parties, the gigantic fall in the membership of trade unions,[15] and the decline in the membership of such associations as the Mothers' Union and Women's Institutes, the British Legion, the Red Cross, and various kinds of youth movements—trends evident in the last decades of the twentieth century.[16] One study of civil society could declare twenty years ago: 'Associations that involve people in the kind of face-to-face interaction thought to build social capital may have been replaced by others that involve little such interaction'.[17]

We may also point to a whole host of other elements and we thereby realise that the concept of 'desocialisation' is an incisive key of interpretation for understanding post-modern society. Increasingly people do not know who their neighbours are and do not interact with them; neighbourhoods are places that increasingly lack points of contact and aggregation (as the decline of the pub well illustrates). Death is undergoing a distancing from social horizons with people dying not surrounded by those nearest to them but alone in hospitals or similar institutions, a development accompanied by the increase in unattended funerals. Good manners as a sign of shared agreement about how to interact with others and maintain social ties have grown weaker.[18] Recreational activity is often engaged in alone—one need only think of the massive levels of surfing on Internet—and the spirit shudders at what the 'metaverse' may bring. And so one could go on.

These are in the main tangible elements but there is also a rather intangible element which is profoundly indicative of the way we live now: the rise of the *lifestyle of selfish individualism*. 'Many people today would claim that they owe nothing to anyone, except to themselves'[19] observed Benedict XVI. There appears to have been a strong shift towards interaction between people becoming increasingly motivated by egotism, with self-interest pervading points of contact. By 1984 an opinion poll reported that 40% of those questioned thought members of their own neighbourhood 'went their own way'; in 2000 this figure had risen to 49%.[20] One of the great points about selfish individualism is not only that it works against reciprocity in personal relationships but also that it acts against taking responsibility for others. Indeed, the current emphasis on 'rights' rather than responsibilities (or to use an old-fashioned word 'duties') forms a part of the dominance of selfish individualism.

The other great feature of desocialisation is 'deculturalisation'; desocialised man is also deculturalised man.

With the decline of an effective context of community (even though there have also been conscious attempts of an ideological kind to 'deconstruct' traditional culture), the cultural inheritance, with all its mechanisms by which to guarantee social cohesion, becomes weakened. The shared manners, mores, morals, customs and habits of that cohesion—and the virtues and principles of life in community as well as other realities—experience a process of debilitation. Given this development it is not surprising that we are witnessing 'traditions in turmoil',[21] to employ the phrase of the Catholic scholar Mary Glendon; indeed, the loss of traditions, far from being an emancipation, can often be an authentic malediction. People find themselves in a sort of no-man's-land where cultural instruments are not to hand for life together in society at a micro- or macro-level. Of course, this process of deculturalisation also implies a removal of the Christian way of thinking and acting that was previously so much at the centre of our inherited way of life. The comment on nihilism of one of the protagonists of Turgenev's *Father and Sons* (1862) is of striking contemporary relevance: 'We shall see how you manage to exist in a void, in an airless vacuum'.[22]

With such developments it is hardly surprising if loneliness now stalks the land. The Labour MP Jo Cox, representing an unusual light of insight in British national politics, was deeply conscious of this scourge and set out to do something about it. The loneliness commission that she founded before she was murdered (in yet another act of horrific violence) produced a report on the subject in 2017. With its highlighting of societal decay, it makes sombre reading. 'Some recent studies have uncovered levels of loneliness across all ages that are worryingly high', it declared, and offered some chilling statistics. Over 9 million adults are often or always lonely. TV is the chief form of company for 3.6 million people aged 65 and over. Over half of parents (52%) have had a problem with loneliness and 21% feel lonely every week. 58% of migrants and refugees in London described loneliness and isolation as their greatest challenge. 43% of 17–25 year olds using the organ-isation 'Action for Children' experienced problems with loneliness. 8 out of 10 carers have felt lonely or isolated because of looking after a loved one. 38% of people with dementia reported losing friends after their diagnosis.[23]

Perhaps the most dramatic feature (and product) of our emerging 'airless vacuum' is the growing epidemic of 'depression'. Many of the children of post-modernity are unhappy children. This is hardly surprising given man's spiritual and biological need for authentic social ties. In the economically highly developed countries, Benedict XVI observed, at the origin of new forms of mental illness 'we may also find the negative impact of the crisis of moral values. This increases the feeling of loneliness, undermining and even breaking up traditional forms of social cohesion, starting with the family institution'.[24] Since 1994 in the UK the number of people 'consulting their GP for depressive disorders has more than doubled, from four million to nine million', it was reported in 1999, and given that 'only half of depressed people actually consult their GP, the real figure is probably even higher'.[25] Concurrently, the number of medical prescriptions for anti-depressants in England rose from nine million in 1991 to 24 million in 2001.[26] By 2017 one in six adults were using these pills.[27] In July 2018 a British national newspaper, under the headline 'Doctors Using Antidepressants to Treat Epidemic of Loneliness', reported that 11% of the age group of 18–24, 19% of the age group of 40–59, and 20% of the age group of the over 60s were prescribed anti-depressants in 2017.[28] In October 2018 it was reported that 'depression' according to UK NHS

data had become the second most common illness diag-
nosed by GPs.[29]

What provokes especial concern is that certain vulnerable groups within society, precisely those groups that
need greatest help, appear to be the particular victims of
these dark dynamics. Statistics on the elderly, the disabled,
children, and the young (not to speak of the unborn—by
2006 a record of nearly 200,000 abortions yearly was
reached in England and Wales: in this ongoing holocaust
of the innocents their deaths destroyed their social ties for
ever)[30] indicate especially high levels of malaise. More than
one in three people aged 75 and over say that feelings of
loneliness are out of their control.[31] The charity 'The Silver
Line' was established in 2013 and now provides a 24-hour
telephone service to the lonely elderly. As of 31 December
2018, this organisation had taken 2.2 million calls over the
previous five years. Its chief executive declared in the same
month: 'I have sleepless nights thinking about what the
demand could be like in two, three or five years' time'.[32]
Childlessness is one principal factor behind such suffering.
In March 2019 it was reported that over a million people
over the age of 65 in the UK were childless (a figure
expected to double by 2030). These elderly were deemed
'dangerously unsupported' and 'at acute risk of isolation,
loneliness, poor health, poverty and being unable to access
formal care'.[33] 50% of disabled people will be lonely on any
given day.[34] 'The NHS in England is helping more than
250,000 under-18s at any one time try to combat their
anxiety, depression, psychosis, eating disorder or other
form of mental illness', reported a national newspaper in
July 2018, 'A quarter of 14-year-old girls are clinically
depressed.'[35] In March 2020, Childline, a telephone service
for children of the National Society for the Protection of
Children against Cruelty, reported that over the previous

three years the number of under elevens calling with suicidal feelings had almost doubled.[36] In early 2019 an opinion poll reported that 18% of young people between the age of 15 and 25 in the UK disagreed that life was really worth living—up from 9% in 2009. More than a quarter disagreed that their life had a sense of purpose. 'Youth happiness levels have fallen most sharply over the last decade in respect of relationships with friends and emotional health, the survey found, while satisfaction with issues like money and accommodation have remained steady'.[37] Cry the beloved country.

Large-scale loneliness has massive economic consequences and huge negative implications for welfare provision by the state. It was estimated in 2017 that loneliness cost UK employers £2.5 billion a year and disconnected communities could be costing the UK economy £32 billion a year.[38] With people increasingly out on their own, and this is especially true of the elderly who have to face a season of life where infirmity is more likely to occur, the question presents itself of how they can be cared for if spouses, family relatives, friends and neighbours are increasingly absent. Government simply does not have the resources to compensate for this shortfall. Where care is not provided in a capillary fashion through inter-personal relationships, social care provided by the state, because of the whole question of cost, simply cannot step in as a remedying force. This of course raises the general question of who should provide 'care' in post-modern society. Pastoral care for loneliness can make a contribution to working against this structural crisis, which in the years to come will become ever more evident to objective observers, and to easing the heavy economic costs of isolation, thereby releasing resources for the fight against poverty and the generation of prosperity: man does not live by bread alone but he cannot live without it. Combatting loneliness is a very sound economic policy.

The great question is what has caused our modern predicament and therefore what its cure is as well: if we know the nature of the illness, we can proceed to treatment. However, reflecting major divisions in Western societies at the level of beliefs, values, and outlook, there are huge divergences in the explanations of a situation which has now become self-evident (even though there remains a frequent reluctance both collectively and individually to recognise and address the problem). These divisions in outlook are of a fundamental nature and point to the growing fading in our societies of a basic shared cultural matrix. Indeed, cultural incompatibilities now form a part of the Western dilemma and underlie rising levels of conflict-ridden political confrontation. According to one opinion poll conducted in the United States of America in July 2018 over 30% of those questioned believed that a 'civil war' was now a very real possibility.[39] Old anchorages have gone and we are now in hazardous unchartered waters. Analysts of contemporary political upheavals in Western societies would do well to see the fading of a basic shared cultural matrix, and the connected realities of desocialisation, as constituting tectonic shifts that are generating seismic tremors and growing fissures within our national polities. Statesmanship, however, seems thin on the ground, not least because there is a lack of comprehension of the fundamental roots of our political malaise. The underlying processes that are working their way through habitually fail to be perceived.

There is good reason to believe that this fading is directly connected to the decline of our ancient faith. This essay stresses the importance of this decline and draws upon Christian faith to explain, analyse and propose a remedy for a cultural crisis that is having truly devastating effects. It shares the diagnosis of the eminent Catholic British parliamentarian David Alton, also an academic and thinker, who in the 1990s launched the Movement for Christian Democracy in the UK.[40] In 2011 he offered these incisive reflections on post-modern British society:

> few mainstream commentators have been willing to make a link between the abandonment of commonly shared Judeo-Christian values and the anarchy which we have witnessed in our institutions and on our streets—partly because for years they have been in the vanguard of attacking those same values as archaic ... A faithless society has become an atomised, lonely, and selfish society; a faithless society has become a culturally diminished society; a faithless society has become a fatherless society and a broken family society.[41]

In another part of the world, St Mother Teresa of Calcutta often stressed that loneliness had become a dominant feature of Western societies, deeming it the most terrible kind of poverty, and she linked this condition to what had happened to Western man at a spiritual and religious level:

> The greatest disease in the West today is not TB or leprosy, it is being unwanted, unloved, and uncared for. We can cure physical diseases with medicine, but the only cure for loneliness, despair, and hopelessness is love. There are many in the world who are dying for a piece of bread but there are many more dying for a little love. The poverty in the West is a different kind of poverty—it is not only a poverty of loneliness but also of spirituality. There's a hunger for love, as there is a hunger for God.[42]

Notes

[1]   An analysis of 'desocialisation'—its causes, characteristics, and
        cure—in Great Britain can be found in my work *Desocialisation.*
        The Crisis of Post-Modernity published in a number of languages:
        Desocializzazione. La crisi della post-modernità (Sienna: Canta-
        galli, 2005); *Desocialisation. The Crisis of Post-Modernity* (Chea-
        dle Hulme: Gabriel, 2009); *Desocializiá. Kríza postmodernity*
        (Bratislava: LUC, 2010); *La désocialisation. Crise de la postmo-*
        dernité (Paris: Du Cerf, 2012); *Desocialización. La crisis de la*
        postmodernidad (Madrid: Encuentro, 2013); *Das Zeitalter der*
        Einsamkeit. Entsozialisierung als Krise der modernen Gesellschaft
        (Freiburg: Herder, 2016). The present essay/manifesto draws
        upon many of the ideas, facts, phrases and quotations of this work
        and forms a follow-up part of the project to which it belongs.
        There is inevitable repetition between this essay and that volume.

[2]   Office for National Statistics, *Social Trends*, 41 (online edition,
        2011), 'Households and Families', p. 4.

[3]   *Ibid.*, p. 6.

[4]   *The Sunday Times Magazine*, 2 September 2007, 'Broken Pieces
        of a Lost Life', p. 24.

[5]   Lord Alton, 'The Condition of England Question—Values and
        Virtues', *Res publica*, 2, January-April 2012, p. 70. In August 2022
        a national newspaper reported that almost a half of children in
        Britain did not stay with both parents throughout childhood,
        with a growing number of young people living across more than
        one household. In addition, one in four families was a headed by
        a lone parent (90% of whom were women), although the figure
        could be as high as one third: *Daily Mail*, 1 August 2022,
        'REVEALED—the scale of family breakdown in modern Britain
        laid bare: Half of children live across more than one household
        and a quarter of families are headed by a lone parent (and 90 PER
        CENT are women), shocking new figures show'.

[6]   A comparison of crime rates in the late 1960s and the late 1990s
        makes dramatic reading: R. Hood and A. Roddam, 'Crime,
        Sentencing and Punishment', in A. H. Halsey and J. Webb (eds.),
        Twentieth-Century British Social Trends (Basingstoke: Macmil-
        lan, 2000), pp. 680–682. By 2017 crime rates were significantly
        lower than their peak in the late-1990s (Office for National
        Statistics, *Statistical Bulletin Crime in England and Wales Year*

Ending December 2017, table 'England and Wales, Year Ending December 1981 to Year Ending December 2017'; available on Internet), but police- recorded crime rates for the same two home countries rose substantially in 2018, reaching their highest level since 2004: *The Telegraph*, 22 February 2019, 'Prosecutions Fall to Record Low—as Crime Hits 14-Year High, Official Figures Show'. Crime rates remain notably higher than the early 1960s.

[7]   Office for National Statistics, *Social Trends*, 33 (London: Stationery Office, 2003), p. 172.

[8]   *Ibid.*, p. 168.

[9]   *The Times*, 20 September 2018, 'No Charges for 90 per cent of Crimes as Violence Soars'.

[10] *BBC news*, 24 January 2019, 'Crime Figures: Violent Crime Recorded by Police Rises by 19%'.

[11] For the dramatic rise in anti-social behaviour 1992 to 2006/7 see Office for National Statistics, *Social Trends*, n. 38, (Basingstoke: Palgrave Macmillan, 2008), p. 128.

[12] *Bloomberg.com*, 9 May 2006, 'UK Has Worst Anti-Social Behaviour Problem in Europe (Update 2)'.

[13] The poll was commissioned by the Centre for Policy Studies: *cps.org.uk*, 22 July 2018, press release, 'New Polling Shows Crisis of Faith in Democracy', with accompanying link to the poll findings 'CPS Survey Results', 7–13 March 2018 (available on Internet).

[14] See M. Fforde, 'The Brexit Referendum: a Popular Revolt of Social Conservatism?', *Studium*, n. 13, May–July 2017, pp. 457–467.

[15] D. Butler and G. Butler, *Twentieth-Century British Political Facts 1900–2000* (Basingstoke: Macmillan, 2000), pp. 141–2, 159, 401.

[16] B. Harrison and J. Webb, 'Volunteers and Voluntarism', in A. H. Halsey and J. Webb (eds.), *Twentieth-Century British Social Trends*, pp. 597, 603, 607, 613.

[17] P. A. Hall, 'Social Capital in Britain', *British Journal of Political Science*, 29, part 3, July 1999, p. 449.

[18] See L. Truss, *Talk to the Hand. The Utter Bloody Rudeness of Everyday Life* (London: Profile Books, 2005).

[19] Pope Benedict XVI, *Caritas in veritate*, 43.

[20] Office for Social Statistics, *Social Trends*, 33 (London: Stationery Office, 2003), p. 21.

[21] M. A. Glendon, *Traditions in Turmoil* (Naples, Florida: Sapientia Press, 2006).

[22]   I. Turgenev, *Fathers and Sons* (London: Penguin, 1975), p. 94.

[23]   Jo Cox Loneliness Start a Conversation, *Combatting Loneliness One Conversation at a Time. A Call to Action* (2017) (available on Internet), pp. 8–9.

[24]   Pope Benedict XVI, *Message for the Fourteenth World Day of the Sick* (8 December 2005) (available on the Holy See web site).

[25]   *The Times Weekend*, 8 May 1999, p. 18.

[26]   Office for National Statistics, *Social Trends*, 33 (London: Stationery Office, 2003), p. 134.

[27]   *The Times*, 21 July 2018, 'Over 70,000 Children Put on Pills for Depression'.

[28]   *The Times*, 21 July 2018, 'Doctors Using Antidepressants to Treat Epidemic of Loneliness'.

[29]   *The Times*, 27 October 2018, 'Depression Overtakes Obesity on GP List of Most Common Illnesses'.

[30]   Office for National Statistics, *Social Trends*, 38 (Basingstoke: Palgrave Macmillan, 2008), p. 26.

[31]   Jo Cox Loneliness Start a Conversation, *Combatting Loneliness*, p. 9.

[32]   *The Daily Express*, 31 December 2018, 'Desperate New Plea to Back Lifeline for the Charity'.

[33]   *The Guardian*, 26 March 2019, 'More than 1m Childless People over 65 are 'Dangerously Unsupported''.

[34]   Jo Cox Loneliness Start a Conversation, *Combatting Loneliness*, p. 8.

[35]   *The Guardian.*, 4 July 2018, 'A Safe Space: NHS Unit on Frontline of Child Mental Health Crisis': 'The last official study of the extent of mental health problems in five- to 16-year-olds, published in 2004 said 10% of that age group had a diagnosable mental health problem. Experts predict an updated version of that report, due in the autumn, will show that the true number is far higher'.

[36]   *Telegraph*, 4 March 2020, 'Childline Sees Number of Under 11s Calling with Suicidal Feelings Almost Double in Three Years'.

[37]   *The Guardian*, 5 February 2019, 'Anxiety on Rise among the Young in Social Media Age'.

[38]   Jo Cox Loneliness Start a Conversation, *Combatting Loneliness*, p. 20.

[39]   *Rasmussen Reports.*, 27 June 2018, '31% Think U.S. Civil War Likely Soon'.

40   This movement contained penetrating insights into what has gone wrong in post-modern British society. For its incisive programme see the leaflet *The Westminster Declaration* ('endorsed by the first national rally of the Movement for Christian Democracy, Westminster Central Hall, November 1990').

41   Lord Alton, 'The Condition of England Question–Values and Virtues', p. 79.

42   Mother Teresa, *A Simple Path*, compiled by Lucinda Vardey (London: Random House, Ebury Digital, 2011), p. 74.

4 DECHRISTIANISATION

A WHOLE SERIES OF thinkers, offering a variety of explanations and solutions, have over recent decades called attention to the breakdown in community which has exploded during the post-modern period in the Western world[1]—the last fifty years or so, exactly the period when secularisation rapidly intensified: the chronology is suggestive of a causal connection. In the 1990s Pope St John Paul II wrote that modern history in the West may be seen as a *'struggle against God, the systematic elimination of all that is Christian'* which 'has to a large degree dominated thought and life in the West for three centuries'.[2] The decline in Christian culture (the outcome indeed of processes which have been working their way through for centuries), and of the core truths it proposes, appears to have played a decisive role in driving people into separation. In reality, a great deal of what has been constructed in an anti-Christian key simply does not work. Yet it is striking that there has been very little inquiry into what the consequences of deChristianisation have been. Might we not be looking at how the West was lost to loneliness? There can be no doubt about the existence of this epochal shift away from our ancient faith. In his *Christifideles Laici* of 1988 the same Pope declared:

> Whole countries and nations where religion and the Christian life were formerly flourishing, and capable of fostering a viable and working community of faith, are now put to a hard test, and in some cases are even undergoing a transformation, as a result of a constant spreading of an indifference to religion, of secularism and atheism. This particu-

larly concerns countries and nations of the so-
called First World.[3]

This is exemplified by the case of Great Britain: during the
nineteenth century one of the most religious countries in
Europe; now perhaps one of the least.[4] Religiosity in societies, as in individuals, is difficult to monitor, but all the
evidence we have points to a retreat from Christian faith:
the decline in going to church on Sundays, marriages in
church, Sunday school attendance, and the importance of
religious questions in politics and denominational loyalties
in determining party allegiances are just some of the
obvious indicators. Opinion polls also help us and certainly
indicate a decline in Christian faith. An opinion poll of a
decade ago put the United Kingdom near the bottom of the
EU table in terms of belief in God.[5] The huge number of
people living alone indicates that post-modernity is something radically new. But so do the very low levels of religious
faith. Are the two phenomena not connected?

It is plausible to believe that the withdrawal of Christian
culture in Great Britain and the West has diminished the
input of the community-building impact of the gospel
message. There is a profoundly socialising drive at the
centre of Christian teaching: God exists, man has a soul,
the soul should be stewarded through love for love and
love for truth which generate healthy spirituality (the
culture of a people should conduce to the same end),
healthy spirituality in turn naturally generates such love,
love for love and love for truth are the essential ingredients
of authentic community at all levels. Here one can see that
spirituality and community have an intimate relationship.
One readily realises that where healthy spirituality fades
in individuals, and where their collective cultures work
against it, where love for love and love for truth are in short

supply, and where the opposite is encouraged, community weakens and loneliness begins to prowl.

However at the centre of the way we think now the idea has become increasingly established that we do not have a soul, something that from a historical point of view has constituted an authentic revolution in thought. Thus from square one there is a lack of a drive, both individually and culturally, to steward the soul and to produce that love for love and for truth that generate authentic social ties: a vital input working for authentic community is removed.

Pope St John Paul II wrote: 'Today an invasive materialism is imposing its dominion on us in many forms and with an aggressiveness sparing no one'[6] and shortly before his election as Pope, Cardinal Ratzinger declared that we are building a 'dictatorship of relativism'.[7] In the place of the Christian spiritual vision of man and its imperatives there has arisen a matrix of materialist visions of man and the related doctrine of relativism. These promote a lifestyle of selfish individualism that acts like acid to break down social bonds and generate behaviour that works against social union. We witness here a precise assault on love for love and for truth—the core gospel message. We are touching upon what has entered the space left vacant by the retreat of the Christian worldview and its concomitant culture—a subject of gigantic historical importance. We are looking at displacement and replacement.

This materialist matrix contains a set of visions of man, all of which deny the existence of God and the soul. 'Humanism' sees soulless man as the supreme pinnacle of a Godless universe; 'rationalism' believes that man must be understood primarily with reference to his rationality; 'animalism' holds that we are only advanced animals; 'sexualism' believes that man is to be defined in terms of his sexual and reproductive impulse; 'societalism' argues that man is a product of society; 'economism' sees us as creatures that struggle after wealth; 'powerism' maintains that we are beings who struggle after power; 'physiologism' holds that we are our bodies; 'feelingism' argues that we are primarily creatures that feel; 'rightsism' believes that man should be seen as the bearer of a set of innate rights; and 'psychism' argues that we are our psyches. Strong elements of determinism and amoralism run through this matrix, as does a propensity to generate competition and conflict. The great drive of these post-modern heresies is to encourage the dark side of man and to promote in him a selfish way of living; in short, to direct him away from the generation and maintenance of authentic community.[8]

Relativism, which holds that truth is a point of view (of individuals, groups, cultures, societies or civilisations), directly attacks love for truth by denying the existence of truth. It is also, of course, a vision of man in that it says that nothing fixed and 'truthful' can be said about what humans are and in this it necessarily counters the Christian spiritual vision of man. Relativism, which has almost become the lode star of post-modern culture in the West, is of course an untenable position and no Western philosopher has ever been able to produce a coherent philosophy of relativism. Relativism not only murders truth, it also murders itself. When applied to itself it disappears, for is the statement 'truth is a point of view' not itself, by its own assertion, also a point of view, and if it is, what then is its value? In attacking truth and all inherited certitudes, relativism, an authentic philosophy of the void, within our civilisation has been a revolution in favour of nothing.[9]

So pervasive are the materialist matrix and relativism that they have left a deep impress on the cultures and the dominant currents of thought of Great Britain and the West. Given what has happened, given the negation of contemporary man, does it not behove the exponents and followers of these currents to reflect on the validity of their approaches and to ask whether their ideas and beliefs really function? More generally, and for the same reason, should not the secularised societies of the West engage in a pause for reflection and ask whether the roads they have taken in recent times have really been the right ones?

'Will we ever succeed', asked the great twentieth-century writer and member of the Russian Orthodox Church, Alexander Solzhenitsyn, 'in giving free rein to the spirit that was breathed into us at birth, that spirit that distinguishes us from the animal world?'[10] The question was well put. The great point about these erroneous visions of man (and of relativism) is that they cannot construct a society that really meets the needs of what we are as humans. As the French Christian philosopher Jacques Maritain observed:

> Materialistic conceptions of the world and life, philosophies which do not recognise the eternal and spiritual element in man, cannot escape error in their efforts to construct a truly human society because they cannot satisfy the requirements of the person, and, by that very fact, they cannot grasp the nature of society.[11]

We should not be surprised that the dominance of such 'philosophies' (and their consequences) means that we have become separated. In his speech to the European Parliament in 2014 Pope Francis had much to say on this process:

> Today there is a tendency to claim ever broader individual rights—I am tempted to say individualis-tic; underlying this is a conception of the human person as detached from all social and anthropolog-ical contexts, as if the person were a "monad"

(μονάς), increasingly unconcerned with other surrounding "monads" ... the rights of the individual
are upheld, without regard for the fact that each
human being is part of a social context wherein his
or her rights and duties are bound up with those of
others and with the common good of society itself
... To speak of transcendent human dignity thus
means appealing to human nature, to our innate
capacity to distinguish good from evil, to that
"compass" deep within our hearts, which God has
impressed upon all creation ... In my view, one of
the most common diseases in Europe today is the
loneliness typical of those who have no connection
with others. This is especially true of the elderly,
who are often abandoned to their fate, and also in
the young who lack clear points of reference and
opportunities for the future ... we encounter certain
rather selfish lifestyles ... A Europe which is no
longer open to the transcendent dimension of life
is a Europe which risks slowly losing its own soul ...
stressing the importance of the family not only helps
to give direction and hope to new generations, but
also to many of our elderly, who are often forced to
live alone and are effectively abandoned because
there is no longer the warmth of a family hearth able
to accompany and support them ... a Europe which
is capable of appreciating its religious roots and of
grasping their fruitfulness and potential, will be all
the more immune to the many forms of extremism
spreading in the world today, not least as a result of
the great vacuum of ideals which we are currently
witnessing in the West.[12]

These words are a call to action. Will the faithful be
capable of responding? One path is the promotion of
pastoral care for loneliness.

Of course, anonymity and non-belonging are also naturally encouraged by mass society. Over the last two hundred

years in the West there has been a move away from small communities, narrow horizons and local variability towards a national social context, distant points of focus and greater sameness. Today, for example, we encounter a giant population, mass politics, a national market, the mass media, large economic units, the big state and mass communications. The symbols of this super scale are huge urban conurbations, massive supermarkets, Internet and being surrounded by strangers. Globalisation is a further step forward on this path and works to construct mass society on a global scale. The problem is that mass society, as E. F. Schumacher, the Catholic author of *Small is Beautiful* (1973), well recognised, despite some obvious positive sides also has an impulse towards the impersonal and the depersonalised. Things are not on a human scale and individuals cannot relate to a context which is simply too big for their need for familiar and accessible frameworks. The consequence is that people increasingly become dots and dots separated from each other. Between mass society and the materialist matrix there is a dark symbiosis and both work massively to objectify man and provoke social distance.[13] 'Are we moving towards an age of colossal organizations and collective institutions', asked the German Protestant pastor Dietrich Bonhoeffer from his Nazi prison during the Second World War, 'or will the desire of innumerable people for small, manageable, personal relationships be satisfied?'[14] T. S. Eliot, the twentieth-century Christian writer and thinker, in his aptly titled (and prophetic) poem *The Waste Land* (1922), in which he wrote that on Margate Sands he could connect nothing with nothing, envisaged a mass society drained of its spiritual and religious content and characterised by the absence of connections:

Unreal City,
Under the brown fog of a winter dawn,

A crowd flowed over London Bridge, so many,
I had not thought death had undone so many.
Sighs, short and frequent were exhaled,
And each man fixed his eyes upon his feet.[15]

Naturally other factors lie behind our present predicament of social breakdown and separation, but in examining the withdrawal of Christian culture, the impact of false visions of man, the corrosive effects of relativism, and the impact of mass society we are probably getting to the causal heart of the matter.

Cardinal G. Müller, who for a number of years led the Congregation for the Doctrine of the Faith, has rightly observed: 'Christianity not only has a future in the Western world of the materialist matrix, it is also the only force that can give the Western world a future'.[16] The true strategy for what has gone wrong, the way to really knit up the unravelled sleeve of community, is a return to a true vision of man and what he is called to do because of his spirituality, a perception of the human soul and its stewardship, a search and respect for truth. If the spiritual bases of community have been weakened or knocked away, then the obvious solution is to restore them to their proper state. In short, a revival of Christian culture in the West, the restoration of that ancient bedrock, in order to generate that love for love and for truth that will restore community to our broken societies. By many routes this will also combat the strength and impact of mass society. The projected 'new evangelisation' of the Catholic Church in this sense is extraordinarily timely. We need to promote the presence of the Kingdom of God amongst us as individuals and cultures; a new divinisation needs to take place. The time has come for Christian renewal—the renewal of our societies and the renewal of Christianity.

It should be immediately observed that at the centre of this re-Christianisation should be the regeneration of the institution of the family. After all, why did Christ bestow a sacrament on marriage? We should put back love between a man and a woman—and between family members, in particular between parents and their children—at the centre of society. Such love is a massive antidote to loneliness and anonymity and this should make us look with great circumspection at ideas and practices that challenge and undermine the family as a living unit. As a part of this, we must adhere to a truthful and constructive view of human sexuality, the nature of masculinity and femininity, and the character of fatherhood and motherhood.[17] Pastoral care for the family is today one of the most pertinent forms of pastoral care promoted within Catholicism and it can certainly link up with pastoral care for loneliness.

This new social ministry can form a part of this new evangelisation and at the same time both carry out Christ's commandments and act to counter the consequences of the fading of faith in our hemisphere. In mobilising the energies of the Church, priests and deacons, Orders and Congregations, public associations of clerics, lay organisations and the lay faithful to help contemporary man in his disaffection, alienation and isolation, pastoral care for loneliness can aid in the regeneration of Western society and the revitalisation of Christianity. Remembering the task of St Francis of Assisi, we can help to repair two interconnected houses.

Notes

[1]   In the United States of America one may cite A. Etzioni and the communitarian movement (for example A. Etzioni, *An Immodest Agenda. Rebuilding America before the Twenty-First Century,* New York: New Press, 1983); R. D. Putnam and his work *Bowling Alone. The Collapse and Revival of American Community* (New York: Simon and Shuster, 2000); J. Olds and R. S. Schwartz and their *The Lonely American: Drifting Apart in the Twenty-First Century* (Boston: Beacon Press, 2009). Overall views of this phenomenon are to be found, for example, in F. Fukuyama's *The Great Disruption. Human Nature and the Reconstitution of Social Order* (New York: Simon and Shuster, 2000), Z. Bauman's *Liquid Modernity* (Cambridge: Polity Press, 2000), and A. Touraine's *Can We Live Together? Equality and Difference* (Stanford: Stanford University Press, 2000).

[2]   Pope St John Paul II, *Crossing the Threshold of Hope* (London: Jonathan Cape, 1994), p. 133.

[3]   Pope St John Paul II, *Christifideles Laici,* 34.

[4]   For a brief analysis of deChristianisation in Great Britain over the last two hundred years see Fforde, *Desocialisation. The Crisis of Post-Modernity,* chap. 6.

[5]   Office for National Statistics, *Social Trends,* 38 (Basingstoke: Palgrave Macmillan, 2008), p. 190.

[6]   Pope St John Paul II, *Agenda for the New Millennium* (London: HarperCollins, 1996), p. 174.

[7]   Cardinal J. Ratzinger, *Homily at Mass for the Election of the Supreme Pontiff* (18 April 2005) (available on the Holy See web site).

[8]   For an analysis of these false visions of man and how they break down social ties see Fforde, *Desocialisation. The Crisis of Post-Modernity,* chaps. 3 and 4.

[9]   For an analysis of relativism and its deeply corrosive impact on social bonds see Fforde, *Desocialisation. The Crisis of Post-Modernity,* chap. 5.

[10]   A. Solzhenitsyn, *Warning to the Western World* (London: The Bodley Head and the BBC,1976), p. 45.

[11]   J. Maritain, *The Person and the Common Good* (London: Geofrey Bles, 1948), p. 70.

[12]   Pope Francis, *Address to the European Parliament, Strasbourg,*

France (25 November 2014) (available on the Holy See web site).

13   For a brief analysis of the rise of mass society in Great Britain over the last two hundred years, and its deleterious symbiosis with materialist visions of man in generating atomisation, see Fforde, *Desocialisation. The Crisis of Post-Modernity*, chaps. 7 and 8.

14   E. Bethge (ed.), *Dietrich Bonhoeffer. Letters and Papers from Prison* (London: SCM Press, 1971), p. 299.

15   T. S. Eliot, *The Waste Land and Other Poems* (London: Faber and Faber, 1972), p. 25.

16   Gerhard Kardinal Müller, 'Gelietwort', in M. Fforde, *Das Zeitalter der Einsamkeit. Entsozialisierung als Krise der modernen Gesellschaft* (Freiburg: Herder, 2016), p. 14 (my translation from the German).

17   See Pope Benedict XVI, *Address of His Holiness Benedict XVI to the Participants in the Ecclesial Diocesan Convention of Rome, Basilica of St. John Lateran* (6 June 2005) (available on the Holy See web site).

5 THE ORGANISATION OF PASTORAL CARE FOR LONELINESS

W HAT FOLLOWS IS a rough blueprint—a provisional programme—for how pastoral care for loneliness could be organised and implemented, a sort of theorisation. Of course many Catholic parishes provide such care as part of their general pastoral activity. Thus the pastoral care committee of the St. John Newman Catholic Church of the Archdiocese of St. Paul and Minneapolis (USA) has the goal of ministry to 'the lonely, the sick, the dying and the families/friends of the deceased'[1] and the Ascension Catholic Parish of Calgary, Alberta (Canada) defines its pastoral care as 'the unconditional caring response to the lonely, shut-ins, the sick and the dying'.[2] The proposal in this manifesto is that given the magnitude of the problem a separate and distinct form of pastoral care should now be developed. This new social ministry will undoubtedly undergo evolution and improvement as it is developed. My feeling is that it is lessons drawn from activity at the grassroots that will really make PCL take off.[3] We are now at its inception and what is suggested here is a modest proposal for what is only a nascent initiative. Indeed, pilot projects of pastoral care for loneliness may be needed to prepare the terrain for a wider launching.

Firstly, there should be a central advisory body that could gather and distribute information, ideas and suggestions for pastoral care for loneliness. It should take advantage of the advances in information and communication technology (ICT) to construct a platform on an Internet web site. It could thus channel all that is good about this new form of pastoral care (for example 'best practices') throughout the world in an ongoing initiative capable of adjustment and development. This platform could be an instrument of input from the grass roots whereby what is learnt and developed at a local level can be fed back to a central collection point where it can then be made available universally. This platform would thus allow a constant upwards and downwards flow. All those directly engaged in pastoral care for loneliness could consult this platform and use it in various ways, not only to obtain and provide information but also to establish contacts and links with people working in the same field. It could also be a point of reference for international Catholic organisations of various kinds, as well as religious Orders and similar bodies, to obtain information on how pastoral care for loneliness could be utilised in their respective special spheres of interest.

This central advisory body could have a special think tank of people expert in the field, of various disciplines, who could dedicate specialised thought to the subject; a sort of academy, perhaps. It could act as a monitoring instrument for the spread and incidence of loneliness and the analysis of the different forms of loneliness and their causes. It could branch out into various areas, such as, for example, the development of a theology (and exegesis) of pastoral care for loneliness, or establishing links with Catholic universities, with the sponsoring of teaching chairs of loneliness studies.

Regional and national bishops' conferences could have regional and national offices for pastoral care for loneliness that could interact with and help PCL at a grassroots level in dioceses and parishes. These offices could link up with the central advisory body and be important channels for the upwards and downwards flow. The use of web platforms, in this process as well, would be of primary importance. These regional and national entities could develop and shape PCL with reference to the special conditions of their respective areas: the kind of pastoral care that is provided could be adapted to the different categories and needs of people in their territories. However, it is the diocese that would be the primary context for the provision of PCL. This would be done through specific teams formed for the purpose, made up, for example, of priests, religious and lay volunteers (some of whom would draw on their own specialist expertise) working either at a diocesan level or in groups of parishes.

But the diocese and parishes would not only be the centre for the practitioners of this pastoral care—they could in themselves, like other ecclesial structures, be a location for the integration and participation of those who suffer loneliness. It should be remembered that for centuries, before the onset of secularisation, parishes and dioceses, often linked to various kinds of associations, offered a powerful instrument by which people were offered face-to-face participation. In thinking about the activities and role of parishes and dioceses, attention should be paid to how they could offer belonging in various forms to those who feel that they are on their own.

'And they went to a place which was called Gethsemane; and he said to his disciples, "Sit here, while I pray." And he took with him Peter and James and John, and began to be greatly distressed and troubled. And he said to them, "My soul is very sorrowful, even to death; remain here, and watch"' (Mk 14:32–34). Christ as he approached his crucifixion asked his apostles to keep him company at a moment of unimaginable travail. Are we not called to keep Christ company in those of our brothers and sisters who are being crucified by massive isolation? It may be that in pastoral care for loneliness one may have to form a special task force for those who find themselves at the far end of the spectrum of loneliness, much as the laudable 'Samaritans' in England constitute a task force by telephone for the suicidal. We have in the West the increasing occurrence of people who are so isolated that when they die nobody knows about the event and notification is only achieved because of the subsequent odour of their decomposing corpses (in Japan the term for these lonely deaths is *kodukushi*). In 2007 *The Sunday Times Magazine* published an article about loneliness ('It seems the UK is becoming a nation of loners') in Great Britain in which it referred to the fate of Andrew Smith, 'one of thousands of people who die alone and unmourned in the UK every year':

> When Andrew Smith died, nobody noticed. His flat, No 171, was at the end of the row on the second floor. His body was discovered when a neighbour, someone he had never talked to, smelt something off and phoned the police. Andrew Smith had been dead for two months ... There were no details on record of next of kin, and nothing in his flat to identify friends or relatives ... he had nobody.[4]

This task force could be called the 'Gethsemanists', drawing inspiration from what took place in that famous garden, and would have to aim at some of the outer fringes of 'society' (if one may call it such) most devastated by the tsunami of the breakdown of social ties. This task force for the chronically isolated would have to have special expertise, capacities and methods because it would deal with very extreme kinds of social isolation. The Gethsemanists could occupy a special position in pastoral care for loneliness and constitute a lineage all of their own. Operating within this pastoral care as a whole, they could nonetheless have their own structures and web sites (or places on web sites) at regional, national and international levels. Perhaps one sees here a Catholic international lay organisation in the making.

A special category of people could be drawn upon by those providing pastoral care for loneliness at a grassroots level, in the same way as their experiences could be used at a variety of other levels to develop the character and effectiveness of PCL. The experience of suffering in life can motivate those who have undergone it to work to ensure that others do not experience it or experience it in a more manageable way. This, indeed, is one of the explanations for the mystery of the existence of evil in the world. Down the centuries, known and unknown holy men and women have been determined to ensure that others do not go through what they went through; pain becomes transformed into compassion. Those individuals defined as 'saints' have often followed this special pathway. Suffering becomes transformed into helping others to avoid or deal with suffering. Those who have experienced loneliness, of a variety of kinds and causes, are especially qualified to participate in PCL: they could bring to bear what they have learned and provide practical wisdom. They are the 'informed' ones who in helping others afflicted by this scourge know what its characteristics and countermeasures are. At the same time, in providing this help they could read what they have gone through in a different and positive light and understand that it was not without a purpose.

Institutes of consecrated life, societies of apostolic life and associations of clerics, especially if they are directed to providing service in the social sphere, could make their own very special contribution to the development of this new kind of pastoral care. It would be fitting for such entities to consider in which way their activities could be directed towards helping the lonely. Those that provide care for the sick could address this category of people, and the same may be said of those who help, for example, children and the young, or migrants, or the poor. They could see in which way the charisms bequeathed to them by their founders could be directed towards the problem of loneliness amongst the categories of people for whom they feel a special responsibility. At a time of increasing difficulties for the future of such institutes, societies and associations, this adaptation of their charisms and traditions to this epidemic of our times could prove a valuable instrument for their revitalisation.

The vast array of lay Catholic associations and movements has a similar opportunity. For example, international federations of these associations and movements are well placed to contribute to PCL. Such federations are often concerned with specific categories of people who could contribute to pastoral care for loneliness or could themselves benefit from it: doctors, nurses, the blind, domestic workers, young people, students, teachers, business executives, and so the list goes on. Here, too, we encounter a possible pathway to revitalisation.

Lay Catholic associations and movements, institutes of consecrated life, societies of apostolic life and associations of clerics have the great advantage for PCL of already having structures that can be activated. They are resources that already exist. ICT and Internet provide potent instruments for that activation. They also provide a channel by which these entities could link up to the central advisory body.

PCL could learn from the other forms of pastoral care that are provided within the ecclesial community, exploring their theological and exegetic bases, seeing by whom and how they are exercised, studying their organisation and looking at their impact. But at the same time PCL could interact and cooperate with these other forms of pastoral care, engaging in a creative symbiosis and leaving its mark upon them. Indeed, PCL is a way of rethinking and calibrating traditional forms of pastoral care in order to make them more suited to the new conditions of post-modern Western societies. Pastoral care for the family, given what is happening in this field, stands out in stark fashion, as does pastoral care for the young.

What we have been talking about in large part in these paragraphs is the mobilisation of organised Catholicism, with a concomitant raising of consciousness, to combat one of the great scourges of our time. What is being proposed here is a very major act of outreach by the Catholic Church to a burgeoning 'fringe' as a response to one of the great signs of our times. We will now turn to the concrete nature of this undertaking. It must be always borne in mind, however, that pastoral care for loneliness aims at two distinct categories whose different profiles have to be taken into account: those within Catholicism and those outside it.

Notes

1   See the web site: www.sjn.org/index.php/parish-leadership /pastoral-care.

2   See the web site: www.ascensionparish.ca/pastoral-care.html.

3   I have greatly benefited from ideas and suggestions expressed to me by people operating at a ground level in response to my talks on desocialisation and what the response of Christians to it should be: for example the seminarians and their teachers of the Community of St. Martin, Evron Abbey, France (28 September 2015); Don Carlo Gestri and the parishioners of the Parish of Paperino, Prato, Tuscany (11 September 2016); Archbishop Graziani and the clergy and lay faithful of the Archdiocese of Crotone-Santa Severina, Calabria (18–19 January 2019).

4   *The Sunday Times Magazine*, 2 September 2007, 'Broken Pieces of a Lost Life', pp. 19, 21.

6 THE CHARACTER OF PASTORAL CARE FOR LONELINESS

W HAT, THEN, COULD be the nature of this new form of pastoral care? I have discussed its organisation, what about its delivery? The focus of the following paragraphs is on the PCL team which could operate at a diocesan level or within a group of parishes and whose various functions as a centre would often overlap. What is presented here is merely a tentative outline as practical experience will inevitably produce new ideas, develop specific features, and offer new pathways. Indeed, it is essential at the outset, as this initiative is developed, to provide input from the grassroots about PCL into the international, national, regional and central points of reference which can then act as sorting offices for feeding positive and constructive proposals back down the lines of communication. Furthermore, as this new ministry develops it will become increasingly clear that there are different categories of the lonely, each with its own configurations and special needs. In addition, varying local contexts, especially of a cultural kind—and this is especially the case as regards areas outside the West—produce their own forms of loneliness and therefore there will be specific related methods for its management and cure. For both these reasons, pastoral care for loneliness will require intelligent calibration by those who provide it. Lastly, in its activity the PCL team can interact with, and draw upon the expertise of, the other forms of pastoral care that are traditionally provided at a local level.

The PCL team should be a *knowledge centre*. Linking up with the central advisory body, the offices of bishops' conferences, religious Orders and similar bodies active in the social sphere, Catholic organisations and lay movements of various kinds that bear upon PCL, and other points of potential input (for example other, but connected, forms of social ministry), the PCL team—in particular through the use of ICT—can acquire and store knowledge of relevance to its purpose. It can thus be engaged in an ongoing process of updating, learning about new research and ideas and the emergence of 'best practices' in its theatre of operations. It can be plugged in to what is going on at a local, regional, national and international level.

In this way, the PCL team can also be a *link centre* of knowledge, a crossroads of connections, but it should extend its network of links beyond the Catholic universe to other Christian denominations, other religions, and the secular world, to central and local government initiatives and to associations, in short, to wherever the question of loneliness is being addressed.

The knowledge handled by the PCL team should include two specific areas: the nature of loneliness and the nature of the impact of loneliness on its sufferer. The character of this malady of modern times should be known about in depth so that fitting cures can be offered; the PCL team should have a clear idea about the nature of the beast. Drawing on a variety of sources and specialist advice, the central advisory body could produce an ongoing compendium to be used by the agents of this new ministry—*Loneliness: a Sufferer's Handbook*. This could address what loneliness is—for example the loneliness of a lack of ties at a personal and domestic level; at a more general social level; and at the level of the overall cultural context in which an individual finds himself. This will help the PLC team to identify what forms of loneliness the people it is trying to help actually suffer from. Such a handbook could also address the psychological impact of loneliness. Studies conducted from a Christian perspective are needed to determine what loneliness does to people at a mental and emotional level so that its symptoms and consequences can be understood. In understanding this impact, individuals will be more able to grasp the realities of their condition and how to manage it.

At the same time, the PCL team can conduct an empirical survey of those living alone, and those suffering from loneliness, in its local area. The results could be a sort of database to help it in its activity. It is interesting in this sense that the British government drew up plans, in the wake of its appointment of its 'minister for loneliness', to obtain information on elderly people by using postmen as the distributors of a questionnaire:

> Britain's 125,000-strong army of postmen and women are set to be given a frontline role in tackling loneliness. Postal workers will be asked to identify and check on isolated elderly people while on their rounds. They will ask a set of questions to collect information about older residents as they are delivering mail and pass the findings to a charity or local authority for analysis. The aim is to link lonely older people with support services or to help members of their family to step in with help. The initiative will be tried out in Liverpool, Whitby in North Yorkshire and New Malden, southwest London. If successful it is likely to be extended.[1]

The PCL team must be an *attracting centre* open to all. The team should be known about so that connections can be established between it and those who suffer from loneliness. Web sites, notices and such literature as bulletins can help to spread knowledge about the team, and the help that it can provide, both inside and outside the ecclesial community. At the same time, its existence can be communicated to a whole range of professional figures, medical doctors or concierges in apartment blocks, for example, who in turn could point out its existence to those who might wish to turn to it. The PCL team should thus be available to initial contacts through such instruments as a web site, an e-mail address, the telephone or a personal visit to its office, all of which can attract the lonely towards the help that it seeks to provide.

In this way, the PCL team can become a *listening centre* for those who approach it. The people received can be listened to, with an identification of their situation, and immediately shown that they are not alone in facing up to what they have to endure. At the same time they can be offered a constructive pathway—and thus hope—by which to deal with the burden that they bear.

This immediate solidarity can then be reproduced by the function of the PCL team of being an *accompanying centre*. Company and presence can be offered to the person who seeks help from the PCL team, and those working with it, either at home or elsewhere. This, in itself, will help to break down that person's isolation and will constitute notable help. 'The Silver Line' charity in the United Kingdom, with its provision of a continuous telephone helpline for lonely elderly people, has demonstrated how constructive this kind of help can be.[2] Through this process of listening and accompanying a dialogue can be opened up on what positive steps can be taken to counter the person's loneliness, with regular discussion about the effectiveness of those steps. An ongoing productive conversation will be proposed.

This forms a part of the PCL team being an *empowerment centre*. Apart from offering specific advice and instruments by which loneliness can be combated, the team can seek to strengthen the people who come to it for aid in a number of ways, all of which can play a key role in countering that great paralyser of action—demoralisation.

Firstly, given the way the West is today, one of the primary features of this pastoral care should be to attempt to show that frequently loneliness and non-belonging are not a result of personal inadequacy but of conditions that are imposed on the individual. This will help the sufferer to counter the stigma that is often associated with loneliness. It was reported in 2017 that in the UK more than one in ten men said they were lonely but would not admit it to anyone.[3] In assessing their state, individuals should realise the kind of society, or in many respects 'anti-society', that they are living in. Given that 'integration' into society is a highly problematic undertaking when there is not that much to be 'integrated' into, full recognition of the surrounding social terrain and its inherent difficulties is of central importance. Individuals who are lonely can often be greatly helped by the explanation to them of what they are surrounded by, and the consequences of their circumstances, with an emphasis placed on the fact that given the way things are in post-modern Western societies loneliness is often imposed on them and not their fault.

Secondly, there is the question of adopting a constructive approach that respects the dignity of lonely people and helps them to look forward. One of the great errors of those providing help to people who suffered from economic poverty was not to respect their dignity and to engage in mere 'charity'. Such an approach involved hand outs and not an attempt to help them manage and move out of their economic distress. This error must not be repeated now in relation to those who suffer from the social poverty of loneliness. What is needed is an approach that strives to value who they are and offer solutions. A vital point is to show these people not only that they can counter and even move out of their condition but also that they are needed, that they can participate and that they can make a contribution.

Such empowerment can also be achieved by reminding those who suffer from loneliness (and believers will be especially receptive to this message) that whatever the social environment may do to them they are not alone. Immediately after his election Benedict XVI declared: 'those who believe are never alone'.[4] What he was telling us is that beyond the human world there are the divine persons to whom we can relate in thought and deed. Communion with the transcendent in a whole host of forms links us to the divine persons who provide us with social ties of a unique kind. Indeed, in interacting with them we interact with those who are always constant and good—they present no risks in the relationships they have with us. Prayer by the lonely is one of the most obvious channels by which to maintain and intensify such links; offering up their sufferings to Christ is another.[5] A relationship with God offers the lonely a powerful way of lessening the impact of their painful corners here on earth.

Along the same lines, the PCL team can tell those who turn to them and are believers that they are connected in a special way with other believers, both living and dead. They constitute a part of a human project that goes backwards and forwards in time. Far from being isolated, they belong to a 'communion of saints' that makes them members of a community with a unique mystical character. Consciousness of such membership, and participation in this communion, provide a sense of being linked to others which shapes an identity all of its own characterised not by isolation but by belonging.

Those who suffer from loneliness can also be strengthened in their trials through a correct vision of themselves and other people. Indeed, ties with God and the communion of saints pre-supposes a perception—and its consequences—that goes against the dynamics of post-modern culture in the West. Man has and is an immortal soul. This is his supreme identity. He should not be seen, for example, as an advanced animal or 'gene machine', or a product of society, or a pursuer of power, wealth or pleasure, or his body or his feelings, but as a spiritual being on an eternal journey. By stewarding their soul through love for love and for truth, lonely people can develop internal spiritual strengths by which to combat isolation and non-belonging. At the same time, they open up to the light of the transcendent and make themselves receptive to that light, thereby gaining strength much as a sunflower obtains energy through following the sun. Equally, they can develop through their spiritual health a natural propensity to reach out to other people which facilitates linking up with others and moving out of their isolation.

This strengthening can be reinforced by a rejection of the idea that truth is 'relative' and by a love and search for truth in all its forms (which is one of the noblest and most ennobling things man can do). The pursuit of truth in relation to themselves, their condition, their purpose and their way forward, with an abandonment of the shifting and confusing sands of relativist thinking, will direct the lonely towards finding ways of coping with and improving their condition.

The PCL team can also be an *aggregation centre* for the lonely and for specific groups of the lonely. One strategy could be the foundation of a special unit to serve as a meeting point for lonely people who can come together to discuss the difficulties they face (and the solutions to them) and receive various kinds of help from the members of the PCL team. A model for this could be the admirable work done by the Archway Foundation of the Anglican St. Matthew's Parish, Oxford (UK) which in significant fashion draws on the contribution of those who have already suffered from loneliness. This foundation was 'established in Oxford in 1982 to help relieve some of the real distress that loneliness can cause. Via social groups and befriending, they connect those feeling alienated, with a diverse group of volunteers, many of whom know for themselves how damaging loneliness can be'.[6]

More specific units or groups could be formed to cater for different categories of lonely people that have their own distinct profiles. Here the list, obviously enough, is not exhaustive. The epidemic of divorce (or the ending of cohabitations) is creating a post-divorce syndrome. People who have lived with another person for years find themselves in the unchartered territory of being on their own and the disorientation of this adds to the loneliness that they may now have to endure. One may also refer to elderly people who for a variety of reasons are now experiencing disturbing levels of marginalisation; or to disabled people who are especially vulnerable to the isolating effects of post-modern culture; or to young people who are very much on the receiving end of the crisis of the institution of the family; or to the unemployed who are cut off from the company of the workplace; or to mothers at home who lack this company but also often find that they do not have relatives near them and encounter a lack of neighbourhood life; or to single parents whose difficulties at the level of isolation are manifold; or to students who often find college life in another city an isolating experience; or to migrants and refugees who for all the invocation of 'integration' find themselves in contexts where there is increasingly not that much to 'integrate' into. Immigration is a major phenomenon of our times, and also a contentious political issue, but it is hardly ever observed that the current loss of social ties in host societies in the West presents migrants with fundamental difficulties at the level of adaptation. In coming together, the members of these groups, and others, can pool their resources, exchange experiences and together with the PCL team generate solutions.

But perhaps above all else the PCL team can be an *advice centre*. Here only some suggestions are made both because of the great variety in the life conditions of the lonely and because as PCL advances it will become clearer what the principal tactics and strategies will be to help people. Much will come out in the wash. The launching of this social ministry is itself an attempt to explore the ways in which loneliness can be combated; it constitutes a research project all of its own.

At various levels the lonely can be advised about their existing relationships and how to make them—where this is possible—a greater source of authentic social input. This is most obviously the case of family relationships, friendships, relationships at the workplace or place of study, and neighbourhood life. What already exists can be built upon to reduce levels of isolation and separation—obviously with all due discernment and caution. Here, of course, the different kinds of pastoral care that are already provided (for the family, for the sick, for young people...) can be utilised and drawn upon to make the advice in this area more effective.

People who are largely confined to the home, because of infirmity, disability or frailty (and this is the condition of many elderly people), can be advised to engage in 'distance' connections through ICT with those with whom they have ties of kinship or friendship, or of other kinds. ICT can also offer them a way of taking part in the world of associations and voluntary work.

Those who do not have such existing relationships can be advised about how to form them where there are the possibilities for doing so. There can be an accompanying of the lonely as they seek to develop social ties in the conditions that surround them.

Voluntary work can be an important and generative form of activity against loneliness because it both offers a sphere of operations for social interaction and also demonstrates the use and value of the person who engages in it. At the same time, the anti-demoralisation effects of helping others (a confirmation that it is 'more blessed to give than to receive': Acts 20:35) can be a potent factor in energising the lonely and leading them to move out of their confines.

At a general level, a powerful way of moving out of loneliness is by helping other people and this should be a central feature of the advice offered by the PLC team to those who turn to them. To share the suffering of others is also to directly link up with Christ who is in those people and thus to engage in a very special tie.[7]

Associations and institutions of various kinds offer major areas of interaction, whether in a face-to-face or online form. These range from political parties to pressure groups, and from professional and labour organisations to associations representing special causes, to name just some categories. In this area the Catholic Church, with its myriad of associations and institutions, offers very promising terrain. Indeed, the incorporation of the lonely into them could prove a potent instrument for their revitalisation. The PCL team could have an updated list of these secular and ecclesial bodies which would be always available for consultation.

At the same time, advice can be offered about ways of engaging in recreational activity or similar initiatives that act as a way of getting people out of the home and of releasing the mind from painfully concentrating on the realities of isolation. It is significant that in July 2018 the British Minister for Health and Social Care responded to news about the mass prescription of anti-depressants for people suffering from loneliness or other mental problems by promising funds for 'social prescribing' schemes. 'Doctors will be able to send greater numbers of depressed patients to gardening and arts clubs rather than automatically reaching for pills',[8] was one national newspaper's interpretation of his declaration.

The PCL team can also provide help to individuals by advising them not to take certain paths that are commonly used to counter loneliness (and which often arise naturally from the visions of man of the materialist matrix outlined above). A frequent feature of how people respond to this form of social poverty, and are encouraged (implicitly or explicitly) by post-modern culture to act to end their isolation, is to choose solutions that in fact only cause them further harm. The adoption of certain 'cures' can in reality only worsen the illness and lead individuals not only back to their lonely starting point but even further back. Leaping from the frying pan into the fire has never helped anybody.

There is a frequent tendency to see the sadness that follows from a lack of authentic social ties as a medical condition that requires medical treatment. Often this sadness is termed 'depression' and its sufferer is led to turn to a medical doctor for help. In the UK three out of four GPs say they see between one and five people a day who come in mainly because they are lonely and one in ten sees between six and ten such patients daily.[9] The result is often the prescribing of anti-depressants and other psychotropic drugs—this can amount to a 'medicalisation' of the problem of the suffering of isolation which, at the level of causes, is in reality not a 'medical' problem at all, even though it is clear that loneliness can have medical consequences.[10] In July 2018 a British national newspaper reported on growing concerns that the nation's doctors were increasingly 'using drugs to combat emotional problems and "medicalising" loneliness'.[11] The real solution is not to treat the body (an approach that reflects the 'physiologist' model of man) but to remove the causes of the unhappiness. I could well put my hand above a flame and anaesthetise it to stop the pain, but the real answer is to put out the flame. Not only is the individual directed down the wrong path and away from possible real solutions, but there is also the very real risk of addiction to such drugs. Needless to say, this prescription of drugs constitutes a major industry for pharmaceutical companies. It may also be observed that pain, as the image of the flame used above indicates, can help an individual to take remedial action (perhaps its cardinal function). The mental pain of loneliness can tell the individual that some-thing is wrong with his situation and that it should be changed. Is it right to remove this important warning signal through psychotropic drugs? What could be a real help to Catholic (and other) doctors is to offer them the possibility of referring their patients suffering from loneliness to a local PCL team. Associations of Catholic doctors at national and international levels could connect with PCL at the same levels to develop this alternative from of response.

Medical doctors as well as prescribing pills to people suffering from the psychological consequences of loneli-ness often direct them to another world. In the West in recent decades there has been a mushroom growth of such practices as 'counselling', 'psychotherapy' and 'mentoring'. We encounter here a kaleidoscopic terrain of all kinds of figures and practices, the presence at times of unproved and debatable theories (not to speak of uncertain consequences and effects), and the frequent request for fees. The help network of family, friends, neighbours, clergymen, workmates and colleagues has been supplanted at times by an impersonal world of very different kinds of figures that is of course permeated by secular post-modern ways of understanding what we are. This world aiming at the purported relief of mental pain is a powerful manifestation of our current predicament. In 1997 a British national newspaper reported on a certain 'Steven' who had received constant 'counselling' from the age of 27:

> I look at it like going to a dentist. I don't have a problem with the stigma, I'd tell anyone. My parents were violent to each other and I learnt to dread hostility; I became a 'pleaser' with violent thoughts. I had a terrible adolescence, I was a depressive with isolationist tendencies. I didn't know how to function in society. I moaned at the therapist for a year, then went into group therapy, which educates you to deal with people.[12]

The army of practitioners of these various forms of 'treatment', like the prescribing of pills, has its obvious risks. Most obviously there is the failure to explain to sufferers that their problems derive from external conditions, for example from an unhealthy cultural context. Instead there is often a tendency to concentrate on 'inner' malfunctions; the 'malady' is said to be within the sufferer. This may be linked to a non-Christian vision of man, through a 'psychist' perspective in particular, that in itself generates errors and cannot see solutions. The PCL team can step in and avoid these failings, as well as others, by being on call to respond to Catholic medical doctors who believe that it can offer more effective help for their 'patients'

Let us also remember the role of nurses. In providing their nursing care they can draw upon, and contribute to, pastoral care for loneliness, addressing the dimension of loneliness of the people to whom they give help. A Catholic international organisation for nurses exists and this could be mobilised to contribute to this development, bringing out the importance of avoiding the medicalisation of the unhappiness caused by loneliness and stressing the constructive help that can be given by the nursing profession, not least through links to PCL teams.

Physiotherapists are increasingly encountering the physical manifestations of the psychological consequences of loneliness. A troubling of the spirit is transferred to the body in various ways because of a somatisation of mental suffering. Catholic physiotherapists, who understand humans—their spirits and their bodies—from a Christian point of view, can provide help in this area. They could be connected to the local PCL team so as to bring their expertise to bear and could be a point of referral for Catholic doctors, supplanting the offering of pills and other 'cures'. There may be room for the creation of a Catholic international association of physiotherapists which could engage with the central advisory council in the scientific study of the somatisation of the suffering of loneliness and the drawing up of responses by this profession to this condition.

Chaplains in hospitals and nursing homes also have a special role to play. In their ministry with the sick and the infirm they encounter people who suffer from loneliness and a lack of social ties, and in the West this is increasingly the case. Chaplains could link up with the PCL team, and receive help from it, in exercising their ministry in a way that can offer special and constructive help to this category of people.

Overall, the world of Catholic health care can make a vital contribution to inverting negative tendencies in the 'treatment' of loneliness and produce a humanisation on a Christian basis of the response of health care to the suffering of isolation, offering a vital input into PCL as this last seeks to grow from being a seed into a tree.

To fill in their emptiness and to change their mood, people who lack authentic social relationships often engage in the pursuit of wealth and power. This can be an attempt to achieve a diversion from personal troubles, to obtain substitutes for companionship and affection, and to secure respect and esteem. An exaggerated commitment to work and what it can bring, for example, becomes a way of burying loneliness and a lack of love. However, this can lead to seeing other people in terms of the economy and power, with all that this implies (the 'economistic' and 'poweristic' traps), and to treating people as objects to be used to obtain rank and material reward. There is also the risk in this strategy that individuals will be surrounded by people who are there because of what they have and not what they are: spouses, companions and friends who are bought are not authentic. There again can the possession of riches and influence on their own ever bring real human fulfilment?

Another erroneous response is to attempt to change the feelings of suffering caused by loneliness through the pursuit of pleasure, excitement and temporary moments of elation: drug consumption, alcohol, excessive eating, gambling, sexual gratification, and endless shopping and consumption all lead a long list of forms of behaviour that in the West have reached epidemic proportions (and link up to 'feelingism'). One of the dangers of this response is that of drugs generally—the need to increase the dose to maintain the same effect, and this becomes a dangerous slippery slope. Another is that the person engaging in such activity will become mightily convinced that the human experience is really about 'feelings', with all that this implies. Hedonism, in this sense, becomes its own self-fulfilling philosophy of life. True pathways to the end of loneliness become obscured and a great deal of damage can be done in the process. Indeed, immersion in these activities can produce behaviour that leads to people being shunned. Alcoholism or drug addiction, for example, tend to alienate others.

Another false cure is to enter into relationships with the opposite sex in order to escape loneliness but without there being a basis of love and affection. Marriages and relationships of this kind are a common feature of post-modernity and a frequent error of our times. The problem is that the other person is being used as an instrument, a means to an end, and thus real authenticity is absent. As love does not exist, true union—the real antidote to loneliness—cannot exist. Indeed, as the relationship does not offer individuals what they really want, they are reminded in stark terms of what they really lack. Further-more, the relationship itself may become a source of stress and strain because its foundations are absent, and it always runs the risk of melting into air. Very similar comments may be made about the formation of artificial and insin-cere friendships. Indeed, the ending of friendships and their transitory quality is as much an increasing feature of the way we live now as divorce in marriage and 'partner-ships' that come and go. Empty relationships can take the lonely back to square one, and even further back.

Another injurious response to loneliness is to create artificial roles and images in order to escape from a human environment that does not provide a sense of belonging and identity. Consolation is sought through invention; individuals become what they are not because their social context does not allow them to be what they are. Isolation and a lack of fulfilment become translated into a playing of parts. Such escapism, however, flies in the face of authenticity and creates relationships that are based on what is false; the phoney and the artificial become pervasive and individuals find again that their social ties are lacking in real content.

Linked to this response is another: not supplied with consideration, respect or esteem by their human environment, individuals are tempted to present themselves in the most favourable light so that they gain admiration for what they are. In deceiving others, they gain gratification from an erroneous perception of themselves. But this engagement in pretence, by denying truth, cannot produce authentic social ties. Of a rather different character is the response of aggression: feeling isolated, neglected and not valued, individuals reject and attack the world around them. At an inter-personal level, it can only compound the problem; if expressed through political ideologies it can be highly destructive of the social fabric.

Lastly, there is the response of self-isolation—withdrawing even more in the face of a social environment that is seen as fundamentally negative. In Japan, where even the idea of robot 'friends' has been mooted (and more widely in the West we have encountered the idea of robot 'lovers'), the term '*hikikomori*' is used to describe this behaviour. People deliberately isolate themselves in order to diminish the painful impact of their social surroundings; a lack of integration leads to a self-removal so as not to experience the loneliness of a world that causes them suffering. This can also involve a flight into a virtual world inside the home with the use of such instruments as the television, downloaded films or Internet. However, this reaction can, in truth, only make matters worse. The illness is being chosen to ward off the illness; the plague is employed to counter the plague.

This is a fitting point to comment on the use of domestic technology as an erroneous response to loneliness, a use not confined to those of the world of *hikikomori*. The growing taste for 'fantasy' in cinema and literature of recent decades forms a part of an escapism prompted by loneliness. The flight into television and DVDs has been known for a long time but the Internet has opened up opportunities in this field on a scale that is truly astounding. The passing of endless hours surfing on Internet (like, at times, activity on social media) places individuals not in face-to-face relationships but in a virtual world fraught with dangers. One classic example is pornography, of which Internet is a gigantic engine. Sexual gratification obtained through looking at the computer screen (or engaging in 'chats') amounts to sex without real human contact, 'desocialised' sex, so to speak, a counter to loneliness which only emphasises the isolation in which individuals find themselves and also exposes the viewer's sexuality to all kinds of risks. The impact of Internet on non-integrated children and adolescents is another part of this new world that is provoking major concern. *Virtually Alone: Pastoral Care for the Cyber Lonely*, a groundbreaking book by the American Lutheran pastor Caleb Crainer, is a recent response to these dangers. The retreat into the domestic world has also given rise to the growing phenomenon of an exaggerated emotional attachment to domestic pets which are treated as though they were somehow humans. This should not surprise us because they are in effect substitute humans. The risks of all these activities should be pointed out by the providers of PCL.

The PCL team can be an *emergency centre* and here the projected Gethsemanists enter the picture. There is a category of people who live in an almost totally isolated state; the Andrew Smiths of this world to whom reference was made above. The grave character of their condition requires special emergency action marked by special methods and approaches. Because of the special nature of the lives of these acute monads, as I mentioned above it may be necessary to develop a special part of PCL that is occupied exclusively with these kinds of people: the lonely with this special profile require PCL with a special profile.

The PCL team can also be a *cooperation centre* and this will help to avoid a ghettoing of this new Catholic social ministry where its exercise is engaged in only behind the drawbridge. Most obviously, the team can work with volunteers who are outside Catholicism but share the goals of its pastoral care for loneliness. The team can also link up and cooperate with initiatives taken to counter loneliness promoted by other Christian denominations; we would here encounter an authentic 'ecumenism of works'. Exactly the same can be done with such initiatives that arise from other religions, and let us never forget the affinities that exist between the world's religions, for example the idea that we have a spiritual principle. In addition, connections could be made with initiatives of the secular world of local and central government and organisations and movements. This cooperation would in itself help to generate understanding, solidarity and community between Catholics and people of different positions in a common cause rooted in humanity; it could help to provoke a cross-fertilisation between diverse points of view; and like PCL more generally it could provide a field for witness with all its credibility-generating potential.

In this section we have talked about the role of the PCL team and how it might operate. But there is another dimension to helping the lonely which involves initiatives organised more generally; a 'macro-background' to this 'micro-activity'. I refer here to three possible initiatives but it will certainly be possible to conceive of many more. They can be taken up in various ways by dioceses and the ecclesial community.

Old people's care homes are at times a symbol of our dysfunctional societies in the West; places where the elderly experience separation and loneliness. One development at an international level has sought to counter this reality. The idea of placing nursery schools in the same buildings as care homes for the elderly, and thereby bringing the elderly into direct contact with children, from whom they can receive interaction and company, began in Tokyo in 1967. Similar schemes (with care homes near to nursery schools as well) were then developed in Europe, Australia, the USA and Singapore, proving of great value and help to the elderly. Nightingale House was the first example in 2017 of a combined nursery school and care home for the elderly in the UK, 'with daily joint activities for the children and residents including exercising, reading, cooking and eating meals'.[13]

The 'homeshare' movement in the UK and other Western countries has sought to counter the loneliness of elderly people, and make renting more affordable, by organising tenancies in the homes of the aged, a strategy much suited, for example, to young people studying at college or working far from the homes of their families. 'Homeshare brings together people with spare rooms', affirms HomeshareUK, 'with people who are happy to chat and lend a hand around the house in return for affordable, sociable accommodation'. 'Recent research by Lloyds Bank Foundation for England and Wales and the Big Lottery Fund', it goes on, 'revealed how inter-generational homesharing can help reduce loneliness and isolation, improve well-being and address the lack of affordable housing options'.[14]

'Independent Age' is an organisation in the United Kingdom dedicated to helping elderly people in a variety of ways. Predictably enough, it pays great attention to the problem of loneliness, offering advice on how to deal with the condition, for example through its guide *If You're Feeling Lonely. How to Stay Connected in Older Age.* It also organises regular visits or telephone calls from volunteers for elderly people suffering from loneliness. Coupled with this is a helpline where an adviser offers information and advice on loneliness to callers.[15]

It may be that through all these activities of this new form of pastoral care to help our brothers and sisters afflicted by loneliness, this way of tending to the afflictions of those who are suffering this malady of our epoch and of keeping Christ company in those who are its victims, this veritable *apostolate for loneliness,* we will hear said to us after our deaths: 'Come, you who are blessed by my Father. Inherit the kingdom prepared for you from the foundation of the world' (Mt 25:34).

Notes

1   *The Times*, 15 October 2018, 'Postmen Asked to Help the Lonely on their Rounds'.

2   *The Daily Express*, 31 December 2018, 'Desperate New Plea to Back Lifeline for the Lonely'.

3   Jo Cox Loneliness Start a Conversation, *Combatting Loneliness*, p. 9.

4   Pope Benedict XVI, *Homily at Mass for Imposition of the Pallium and Conferral of the Fisherman's Ring at the Beginning of the Petrine Ministry of the Bishop of Rome* (24 April 2005) (available on the Holy See web site). Benedict XVI also described this phrase as the 'motto' of his journey to Bavaria of 14–19 September 2006: Benedetto XVI, *Chi crede non è mai solo* (Sienna: Cantagalli, 2006), p. 43.

5   See Rm 8:17; Col 1:24; Pope St John Paul II, *Salvifici Doloris*, 26.

6   See the web site: *www.archway foundation.org.uk*.

7   This was a point repeatedly made by the clergy, religious and lay faithful who took part in the symposium held in Calabria in January 2019 on the possibility of launching pastoral care for loneliness within the Catholic world.

8   *The Times.co.uk*, 23 July 2018, 'Doctors Urged to Offer more Gardening Courses and Fewer Pills'.

9   Jo Cox Loneliness Start a Conversation, *Combatting Loneliness*, p. 10.

10   For an important contribution to the subject see J. J. Lynch, *The Broken Heart: the Medical Consequences of Loneliness* (Sydney: Harper and Row, 1977).

11   *The Times*, 21 July 2018, 'Doctors Using Antidepressants to Treat Epidemic of Loneliness'.

12   *The Sunday Times Magazine*, 5 Jan. 1997, p. 41.

13   *The Guardian*, 6 September 2017, '"It's Like Being Reborn": Inside the Care Home Opening its Doors to Toddlers'.

14   See the web site of 'HomeshareUK. The UK Network for Home-share': *homeshareuk.org*.

15   See the web site of 'Independent Age': *independentage.org*, especially 'Loneliness' in the 'Personal life' section.

BIBLIOGRAPHY

Church documents

Vatican Council II, *Gaudium et Spes* (1965).

Pope St John Paul II, *Salvifici Doloris* (1984).

Pope St John Paul II, *Christifideles Laici* (1988).

Pope St John Paul II, *Crossing the Threshold of Hope* (London: Jonathan Cape, 1994).

Catechism of the Catholic Church (London: Geoffrey Chapman, 1994).

Pope St John Paul II, *Agenda for the New Millennium* (London: HarperCollins, 1996).

Pope Benedict XVI, *Homily at Mass for Imposition of the Pallium and Conferral of the Fisherman's Ring at the Beginning of the Petrine Ministry of the Bishop of Rome* (24 April 2005).

Pope Benedict XVI, *Address to the Participants in the Ecclesial Diocesan Convention of Rome, Basilica of St. John Lateran* (6 June 2005)

Pope Benedict XVI, *Message for the Fourteenth World Day of the Sick* (8 December 2005).

Benedetto XVI (Pope Benedict XVI), *Chi crede non è mai solo* (Sienna: Cantagalli, 2006).

Pope Benedict XVI, *Caritas in veritate* (2009).

Pope Francis, *General Audience* (5 June 2013).

Pope Francis, *Evangelii Gaudium* (2013).

Pope Francis, *Message for the Twenty-Ninth World Youth Day 2014* (21 January 2014).

Pope Francis, *Address at the Conclusion of Luncheon with the Participants in the International Seminar on the Pope's Proposal 'Towards a More Inclusive Economy' Made in the Apostolic Exhortation* Evangelii Gaudium (12 July 2014).

Pope Francis, *Address to the European Parliament, Strasbourg, France* (25 November 2014).

Pope Francis, Apostolic Journey to Sri Lanka and the Philippines (12–19 January 2015), *Address to Families* (16 January 2015).

Pope Francis, *Address to the Members of the National Association of Italian Municipalities (ANCI)* (30 September 2017).

Pope Francis, *Message to the Executive Chairman of the "World Economic Forum" on the Occasion of the Annual Gathering in Davos-Klosters* (12 January 2018).

Pope Francis, *Address to the Emmanuel Community* (7 April 2018).

Cardinal P. Parolin, *Thanksgiving Mass for the Canonisation of Mother Teresa: Eyes Open to Suffering, Embraced with Compassion* (5 September 2016).

Cardinal J. Ratzinger, *Homily at Mass for the Election of the Supreme Pontiff* (18 April 2005).

Books

Z. Bauman, *Liquid Modernity* (Cambridge: Polity Press, 2000).

E. Bethge (ed.), *Dietrich Bonhoeffer. Letters and Papers from Prison* (London: SCM Press, 1971).

F. Bound Alberti, *A Biography of Loneliness: the History of an Emotion* (Oxford: Oxford University Press, 2019).

D. Butler and G. Butler, *Twentieth-Century British Political Facts 1900–2000* (Basingstoke: Macmillan, 2000).

C. J. Calipeau, *Isaiah Berlin's Liberalism* (Oxford: Clarendon Press, 1994).

C. Crainer, *Virtually Alone: Pastoral Care for the Cyber Lonely* (Kindle Edition, 2017).

T. S. Eliot, *The Waste Land and Other Poems* (London: Faber and Faber, 1972).

A. Etzioni, *An Immodest Agenda. Rebuilding America before the Twenty-First Century* (New York: New Press, 1983).

M. Fforde, *Desocialisation. The Crisis of Post-Modernity* (Cheadle Hulme: Gabriel, 2009).

F. Fukuyama, *The Great Disruption. Human Nature and the Reconstitution of Social Order* (New York: Simon and Shuster, 2000).

M. A. Glendon, *Traditions in Turmoil* (Naples, Florida: Sapientia Press, 2006).

M. Harris, *Culture, People, Nature. An Introduction to General Anthropology* (New York: Harper and Row, 1980).

Jo Cox Loneliness Start a Conversation, *Combatting Loneliness One Conversation at a Time. A Call to Action* (2017) (available on Internet).

J. J. Lynch, *The Broken Heart: the Medical Consequences of Loneliness* (Sydney: Harper and Row, 1977).

J. Maritain, *The Person and the Common Good* (London: Geofrey Bles, 1948).

Office for National Statistics, *Social Trends*, 33 (London: Stationery Office, 2003).

Office for National Statistics, *Social Trends*, 38 (Basingstoke: Palgrave Macmillan, 2008).

Office for National Statistics, *Social Trends*, 41 (online edition, 2011).

J. Olds and R. S. Schwartz, *The Lonely American: Drifting Apart in the Twenty-First Century* (Boston: Beacon Press, 2009).

R. D. Putnam, *Bowling Alone. The Collapse and Revival of American Community* (New York: Simon and Schuster, 2000).

A. Solzhenitsyn, *Warning to the Western World* (London: The Bodley Head and the BBC, 1976).

Mother Teresa, *A Simple Path*, compiled by Lucinda Vardey (London: Random House, Ebury Digital, 2011).

A. Touraine, *Can We Live Together? Equality and Difference* (Stanford: Stanford University Press, 2000).

L. Truss, *Talk to the Hand. The Utter Bloody Rudeness of Everyday Life* (London: Profile Books, 2005).

I. Turgenev, *Fathers and Sons* (London: Penguin, 1975).

Articles

Lord Alton, 'The Condition of England Question—Values and Virtues', *Res Publica*, 2, January–April 2012, pp. 63–79.

BBC.com/news/UK, 24 Jan. 2019, 'Crime Figures: Violent Crime Recorded by Police Rises by 19%'.

Bloomberg.com, 9 May 2006, 'UK Has Worst Anti-Social Behaviour Problem in Europe (Update 2)'.

The Centre for Policy Studies, 'New Polling Shows Crisis of Faith in Democracy' (available on Internet: *cps.org.uk*, 22 July 2018).

The Daily Express, 31 December 2018, 'Desperate New Plea to Back Lifeline for the Lonely'.

The Daily Mail, 1 August 2022, 'REVEALED—the scale of family breakdown in modern Britain laid bare: Half of children live across more than one household and a quarter of families are headed by a lone parent (and 90 PER CENT are women), shocking new figures show'.

The Daily Telegraph, 22 February 2019, 'Prosecutions Fall to Record Low—as Crime Hits 14-Year High, Official Figures Show'.

The Daily Telegraph., 4 March 2020, 'Childline Sees Number of Under 11s Calling with Suicidal Feelings Almost Double in Three Years'.

M. Fforde, 'The Brexit Referendum: a Popular Revolt of Social Conservatism?', *Studium*, n. 13, May-July 2017, pp. 457–467.

The Guardian, 6 September 2017, "It's Like Being Reborn': Inside the Care Home Opening its Doors to Toddlers'.

The Guardian, 16 January 2018, 'May Appoints Minister to Tackle Loneliness Issues Raised by Jo Cox'.

The Guardian, 5 February 2019, 'Anxiety on Rise among the Young in Social Media Age'.

The Guardian, 26 March 2019, 'More than 1m Childless People over 65 are 'Dangerously Unsupported''.

The Guardian, 4 July 2018, 'A Safe Space: NHS Unit on Frontline of Child Mental Health Crisis'

P. A. Hall, 'Social Capital in Britain', *British Journal of Political Science*, 29, part 3, July 1999, pp. 417–461.

B. Harrison and J. Webb, 'Volunteers and Voluntarism', in A. H. Halsey and J. Webb (eds.), *Twentieth-Century British Social Trends* (Basingstoke: Macmillan, 2000), pp. 587–619.

R. Hood and A. Roddam, 'Crime, Sentencing and Punishment', in A. H. Halsey and J. Webb (eds.), *Twentieth-Century British Social Trends,* pp. 675–709.

E. M. Marginean, 'Transforming Loneliness: An Orthodox Christian Answer to an Increasing Loneliness in Disabled Populations', *Religions* 13:9 (2022), pp. 863–871.

Gerhard Kardinal Müller, 'Gelietwort', in M. Fforde, *Das Zeitalter der Einsamkeit. Entsozialisierung als Krise der modernen Gesellschaft* (Freiburg: Herder, 2016), pp. 7–14.

Office for National Statistics, *Statistical Bulletin Crime in England and Wales Year Ending December 2017.*

Rasmussenreports.com, 27 June 2018, '31% Think U.S. Civil War Likely Soon'.

The Sunday Times Magazine, 2 Sept. 2007, 'Broken Pieces of a Lost Life'.

The Times, 21 July 2018, 'Over 70,000 Children Put on Pills for Depression'.

The Times, 21 July 2018, 'Doctors Using Antidepressants to Treat Epidemic of Loneliness'.

The Times, 23 July 2018, 'Doctors Urged to Offer more Gardening Courses and Fewer Pills'.

The Times, 20 Sept. 2018, 'No Charges for 90 per cent of Crimes as Violence Soars'.

The Times, 15 October 2018, 'Postmen Asked to Help the Lonely on their Rounds'.

The Times, 27 October 2018, 'Depression Overtakes Obesity on GP List of Most Common Illnesses'.

The Westminster Declaration ('Endorsed by the first national rally of the Movement for Christian Democracy, Westminster Central Hall, November 1990').